Theodor SEUSS Geisel

LIVES AND LEGACIES

———

Larzer Ziff
MARK TWAIN

David S. Reynolds
WALT WHITMAN

Edwin S. Gaustad
ROGER WILLIAMS
BENJAMIN FRANKLIN

Gale E. Christianson
ISAAC NEWTON

Paul Addison
CHURCHILL: THE UNEXPECTED HERO

G. Edward White
OLIVER WENDELL HOLMES JR.

Craig Raine
T. S. ELIOT

Carolyn Porter
WILLIAM FAULKNER

Donald E. Pease
THEODOR SEUSS GEISEL

Theodor SEUSS Geisel

Donald E. Pease

OXFORD
UNIVERSITY PRESS
2010

OXFORD
UNIVERSITY PRESS

Oxford University Press, Inc., publishes works that further
Oxford University's objective of excellence
in research, scholarship, and education.

Oxford   New York
Auckland   Cape Town   Dar es Salaam   Hong Kong   Karachi
Kuala Lumpur   Madrid   Melbourne   Mexico City   Nairobi
New Delhi   Shanghai   Taipei   Toronto

With offices in
Argentina   Austria   Brazil   Chile   Czech Republic   France   Greece
Guatemala   Hungary   Italy   Japan   Poland   Portugal   Singapore
South Korea   Switzerland   Thailand   Turkey   Ukraine   Vietnam

Copyright © 2010 by Donald E. Pease

The images on pages 7, 8, 21, 55, 60, 82, 84, 86–90, 95, 98, 105–7, 110, 116, 119–20, 123–24, 126, 139–40, 144–45, and 151 are reprinted courtesy of Random House. The images on pages 28–32, 37, and 42 are reprinted courtesy of the Rauner Library. The images on pages 62 and 65–67 are reprinted courtesy of *PM*. The images on pages 45, 47, and 53 are reprinted courtesy of *Judge*. The image on page 43 is reprinted courtesy of the *Saturday Evening Post*.

Published by Oxford University Press, Inc.
198 Madison Avenue, New York, New York 10016

www.oup.com

Oxford is a registered trademark of Oxford University Press

Library of Congress Cataloging-in-Publication Data
Pease, Donald E.
Theodor Seuss Geisel / Donald E. Pease.
p.   cm. — (Lives and legacies)
Includes bibliographical references and index.
ISBN 978-0-19-532302-3
1. Seuss, Dr. 2. Authors, American—20th century—Biography.
3. Illustrators—United States—Biography.
4. Children's literature—Authorship. I. Title.
PS3513.E2Z794 2010
813'.52—dc22
[B]   2009036478

7   9   8

Printed in the United States of America
on acid-free paper

For Thomas Alexander Pease (1955–2008),
who grew up reading Dr. Seuss;
Marie Theresa Giebel Pease (1924–1999),
who made it all fun;
and Patricia McKee,
who added the cats

Contents

Preface

In the course of his sixty-five-year career, Theodor Seuss Geisel was an advertisement agency artist, animator, producer and director of animated cartoons, caricaturist, playwright, short story writer, documentary filmmaker, lyricist, teacher, political cartoonist, and editor and author of children's books. Early in his career he invented the persona of Dr. Seuss to integrate these disparate facets of his creative personality. But Dr. Seuss did not wholly commit himself to authoring books for children until the 1950s.

Dr. Seuss's children's books have enjoyed phenomenal commercial and critical success. Dr. Seuss's works, which have changed the way children everywhere learn how to read, have been translated into fifteen languages. More than 200 million copies of his books have been sold worldwide. Six books have been published posthumously. In 2001 *Publishers Weekly* listed fourteen Dr. Seuss books among the top one hundred all-time best-selling hardcover children's books. *Green Eggs and Ham* placed fourth on the list, and *The Cat in the Hat* ranked ninth. They were followed by *One fish two fish red fish blue fish* (13), *Hop on Pop* (16), *Oh, the Places You'll Go!* (17), *Dr. Seuss's ABC* (18), *The Cat in the Hat Comes Back* (26), *Fox in Socks* (31), *How the Grinch Stole Christmas!* (35), *My Book About Me* (40), *I Can Read with My Eyes Shut!* (58), *Oh, the Thinks You Can Think!*

(65), *Oh Say Can You Say?* (85), and *There's a Wocket in My Pocket!* (93). The number of best-sellers rises to twenty-six when the list is extended to the top 189.

During his lifetime his work was awarded two Oscars, two Emmys, a Peabody, a New York Library Literary Lion, three Caldecott Honor Awards, and a Laura Ingalls Wilder Award. In 1999 the Cat in the Hat's face was placed on a 33 cent U.S. stamp. The Dr. Seuss National Memorial in Springfield, Massachusetts, which was designed by his stepdaughter Lark Grey Dimond-Cates, opened in 2002. In 2004 a U.S. stamp with Theodor Seuss Geisel's portrait appeared. In that same year he received a star on the Hollywood Walk of Fame.

Several important works on Dr. Seuss's voluminous legacy have appeared in the past twenty years. Ruth MacDonald published the first comprehensive commentary on his children's books in 1988. Eleven years later Richard H. Minear published a book entitled *Dr. Seuss Goes to War*, in which he convincingly explains Dr. Seuss's political turn. Philip Nel's 2004 volume, *Dr. Seuss: American Icon*, resituates Dr. Seuss's project within a post-modern context. In *The Seuss, the Whole Seuss and Nothing but the Seuss: A Visual Biography of Theodor Seuss Geisel*, which was also published in 2004, Charles Cohen provides an indispensable study of the relationship between the figures in Dr. Seuss's children's books and the images and verse he composed during his early years as a cartoonist and advertising artist. These scholars have taught us a lot about the man's legacy and his life, but they have not engaged the question of the relationship between Dr. Seuss's art and Geisel's life. This book for Oxford's Lives and Legacies Series constitutes a modest effort to explore this relationship.

In preparation for their authoritative 1995 biography, *Dr. Seuss and Mr. Geisel,* Judith and Neil Morgan asked Geisel how he produced his children's books. Geisel replied that he liked to approach a book with a situation or a conflict and then write himself into an impossible position "so there was seemingly no way of ending the book." Then he tried to find a way out. The seemingly erratic transitions of Geisel's artistic career bear a close resemblance to the zigzag plot lines of his children's books. To keep track of the significance of such transitions, I have organized this account of the relationship between Geisel's life and Dr. Seuss's art around decisive turning points. Each of the chapters focuses on a specific event or on particular works that illustrated the intertwining of the life and the art.

The complexity at work in this relationship required that I establish a logic governing when to use "Ted," "Geisel," and "Dr. Seuss" in naming the protagonist of specific actions. "Ted" is the name for the child who grew up in Springfield and went on to Dartmouth to study; the name is meant to convey the intimacy of a classmate, husband, and brother. "Geisel" names the mature man whose growing success supplied the objective understanding required to decide on the changes in the trajectory of the career. "Dr. Seuss" refers to the creative personality Geisel designated as the author of the children's books. When he assumed the persona of the children's book writer as his primary identity, Dr. Seuss endowed Geisel's other personae with a new orientation.

THEODOR SEUSS GEISEL

One

DR. SEUSS'S PASSAGE HOME

In 1936 Theodor Seuss Geisel was returning from Germany, his grandparents' ancestral homeland, aboard the luxury ocean liner the MS *Kungsholm*. Out in the North Atlantic a summer storm began battering the ship with gale-strength winds. Waves rocked the ship with such force that the officers ordered passengers to return to their cabins. Geisel worried whether he and his wife would survive the trip.

He had been only eight years old when the *Titanic* sank off the coast of Newfoundland on April 15, 1912, and eleven when German submarines torpedoed the *Lusitania*, killing 1,198 people. Sensational newspaper accounts of these disasters at sea were deeply etched in childhood memories that included his watching a float used in the Springfield, Massachusetts, 4th of July parade in 1912, which he later described in mock-epic rhyme:

Dragged by two teams of sweating stallions
Down Main Street the cardboard iceberg lurched.
And on the top deck of the sinking Titanic
A brave stringed quartette precariously was perched.[1]

After becoming seasick and claustrophobic Geisel tried to get his mind off the storm by heading to the ship's lounge, where his seasickness gave way to homesickness. On a sheet of the *Kungsholm*'s stationery he scribbled a series of loosely associated variations on the image of a horse-drawn carriage that he recalled from his youth.

A stupid horse and wagon
Horse and chariot
Chariot pulled by flying cat
Flying cat pulling Viking ship[2]

Geisel proceeded to imagine himself contributing to the ship's ability to withstand the storm by writing verses whose anapestic rhythm duplicated the engine's chugging sound. The lines also matched the cadence of "Twas the Night Before Christmas": "And that is a story that no one can beat, / And to think that I saw it on Mulberry Street."[3]

Springfield: Ted Geisel's Hometown

The last two words of the second line refer to one of the main thoroughfares in the city where Geisel spent the first eighteen years of his life. His roots reached back into Bavaria by way of Springfield, Massachusetts. From his birth at 22 Prospect Street on March 2, 1904, to his death in La Jolla, California, on September 24, 1991, Geisel's life was marked by the major events of the twentieth century. Although he was born into one of the most prosperous families in Springfield, from an early age he learned how to cope with social and economic misfortune.

In the early years of the twentieth century Springfield transformed itself from a provincial frontier town into the largest manufacturing center north of Boston, featuring an armory and dozens of buildings connected to the emergent cotton and steel industries. The town's population doubled in size, from forty-four thousand in 1890 to eighty-eight thousand in 1910. Five railroad lines dispatched more than two hundred trains through Springfield each day to transport people and goods to New York City and throughout New England. A comparably large number of barges and steamboats were busy servicing its seaport.

These massive changes posed significant challenges to the powers of adaptation of Springfield's citizens. Those who knew how to take advantage of the new economic opportunities prospered. They built Hudson cars, machine parts, Knox and Duryea engines, Indian motorcycles, and Smith and Wesson rifles. They purchased G. and C. Merriam dictionaries, played Milton Bradley games, and learned the rules of Naismith ball (as basketball was called, after its inventor). Members of Springfield's large immigrant communities also contributed to the city's makeover as a thriving metropolis.

Geisel's grandfather, also named Theodor Geisel, had emigrated from Germany in 1867 and was justly proud of the affluence and social standing that he had achieved through hard work and shrewd investments. Born in 1840 in the Baden town of Muehlhausen, he learned his trade as a jeweler's apprentice and fought in the cavalry during Germany's seven-week war with Austria. He sailed to America to join friends in Springfield as a jeweler specializing in brooches and pendants. In 1871 he married Christine Schmaelzle, and in 1874 he became a U.S. citizen. Two years later he pooled resources with a fellow German immigrant named Christian Kalmbach and founded a small brewery.

Arms manufacture and breweries ranked high among the industries for which Springfield had acquired its reputation. The Geisel household had an interest in both. The Kalmbach and Geisel Brewery became one of the most successful in Springfield, competing with breweries in New York and Boston. Over the years Theodor Geisel acquired several choice pieces of Springfield real estate and developed a large circle of friends in the German community.

On June 28, 1879, Geisel's father, Theodor Robert (T. R.) Geisel, was born in the house next door to the brewery. T. R. grew up to share his father's wish to improve the family's standing in the community. The most proficient rifle marksman in New England, he became a member of the Fraternal and Benevolent Order of Elks, president of the Springfield Kiwanis, an incorporator of the Hampden County Bank, and a lifelong member of the Hampden Republican Party. He was also a major in the State Guard and liked being addressed by that title. In 1904 T. R. was named a member of the Springfield Board of Parks, and five years later he was elected its commissioner. He ran an unsuccessful campaign for mayor in 1929.

His marriage to Henrietta Seuss in 1901 strengthened the Geisel family's ties to the local German community. Henrietta, known as Nettie, was the daughter of George Seuss, the owner of the Seuss Bakery and founding president of the Springfield Turnverein, a social and gymnastics club that was the hub of the German American community. After his marriage T. R. renounced his family's Catholicism and joined Nettie's Lutheran church.

By 1915 the German American community in Springfield included twelve hundred adults and five thousand children with at least one German parent. The Turnverein Gymnastic Hall, the Trinity Evangelical Lutheran Church, and the Schuetzenverein Rifle Club—of which Geisel's paternal grandfather was a founding member—all offered their services in German. The Court Square Theater staged events with German songs and food. Evidence of the contribution of German culture to the city's betterment could be found on the pediments and lintels of libraries, concert halls, athletic unions, and businesses throughout Springfield. On Saturdays the Geisels would join their German friends to wash down Boston beans and bratwurst with numerous bottles of the family beer. Each Christmas the Geisels and the Seusses gathered with other members of the German community to sing "Stille Nacht" and "O Tannenbaum."[4]

The family had a quasi-proprietary relation to Springfield's entertainment industries. Geisel's grandfather distributed the beer and spirits, and his father supervised its parks and picnic areas. The Kalmbach and Geisel Brewery possessed the dignity of one of Springfield's established institutions. It provided the Geisels with their livelihood as well as their social standing. Each change of the brewery's name—from Kalmbach and Geisel Springfield Brewery Company to the Highland Brewing Company in 1895, to the Liberty Brewing Company in 1901—attested to the family's desire to assimilate. By the time the Liberty Brewing Company merged with Springfield Breweries in 1920 sales from Geisel-owned breweries had grown to more than 300,000 barrels a year.[5]

T. R.'s inventiveness, enterprise, and self-discipline won him the respect of the Springfield business community, though he had a taciturn demeanor. Geisel remembered his father saying, "You will never be sorry for anything you never said."[6] Ted did not adopt his father's habits of self-regimentation. He disliked the gymnastic lessons his father compelled him to take at Turn-verein, where he also learned rope climbing and calisthenic leaps. He developed an aversion to hunting and marksmanship, and he hated wearing pink jersey shirts and pumps for the dancing classes he was forced to take at the Hotel Kimball.

The German community commemorated T. R.'s marriage to Henrietta Seuss with a widely circulated folk saying that expressed its different valuations of the Seuss and Geisel families: "Seuss the baker puts the staff of life in people's mouths. Geisel the brewer takes it out and pours beer there instead, causing the children of drinkers to suffer the pangs of hunger."[7]

"Was There Nothing to Look at . . . No People to Greet?"

In response to questions about the origins of his art, Geisel later named as its primary source his boyhood in Springfield: "Why write about Never-Never Lands that you've never seen—when all around—you have a Real Never-Never Land that you know about and understand."[8] It is fitting, then, that for the remainder of the tumultuous Atlantic crossing, Geisel could get neither the engine's anapests nor Mulberry Street out of his head. After they disembarked his wife encouraged him to develop a story line combining the two. The need to recapture the excitement out of which the lines originated inspired Geisel to create an illustrated narrative in verse whose momentum would keep children turning the pages. Johnson's Bookstore in Springfield was one of the first book-shops to which Vanguard Press distributed copies of the finished book, *And to Think That I Saw It on Mulberry Street*, in the fall of 1937. But many of the residents who lined up outside

Johnson's to purchase it expressed anxiety over Geisel's depiction of their hometown.[9] The relationship between the Geisels and their Springfield neighbors had not always been a cordial one.

The story opens with a scene of paternal instruction. Marco's father directs him to report what he observes on his way to and from school along Mulberry Street, but simultaneously warns him against indulging his penchant for exaggeration:

"Marco, keep your eyelids up
And see what you can see."
But when I tell him where I've been
And what I think I've seen,
He looks at me and sternly says,
"Your eyesight's much too keen.
Stop telling such outlandish tales
Stop turning minnows into whales."[10]

Marco nonetheless finds it impossible to give up inventing impressive variations on what he sees. The first sight he comes upon is a nondescript wagon drawn by a bedraggled horse and a bemused driver, which Marco dismisses with the remark that this is "nothing to tell of." Then he imagines a series of increasingly spectacular modifications to this street scene, which culminates in

a "rajah with rubies perched high on a throne" on top of a blue elephant, who, along with giraffes and a motorcycle police escort, is transporting a huge brass band and trailer past the mayor's viewing platform, as two men standing on the wings of an airplane passing overhead pour confetti down on the procession. This improbable tableau dramatizes the motive for Marco's tale. Each fantastic substitution allows him to postpone the anticipated humiliation and shame that take place in the book's concluding scene:

> Dad looked at me sharply and pulled at his chin.
> He frowned at me sternly from there in his seat,
> "Was there nothing to look at . . . no people to greet?
> Did *nothing* excite you or make your heart beat?"
> "Nothing," I said, growing red as a beet,
> "But a plain horse and wagon on Mulberry Street."

Marco's story emerges in response to his father's scolding. After the opening scene, however, he shifts the audience from his father to the implied readers, who know how to turn his tall tales into pleasure. These readers differ from Marco's father because they want to believe in the fantasy that Marco creates.

MOTHER SEUSS

Geisel coped with his rough passage home from Germany by writing a children's book that took him back to his early years, but the story did not merely return him to his Springfield childhood. Geisel reentered his childhood through the intervention of a persona, Dr. Seuss, who endowed the past with a promising future. Dr. Seuss's story intertwined Geisel's adult anxieties about a dangerous Atlantic crossing with Marco's emotional turmoil during his walk home. *And to Think That I Saw It on Mulberry Street* also adds the figures that Geisel's actual childhood lacked. Springfield became the template for a second world, the creation of which helped Geisel come to terms with his childhood.

When Marco runs up the stairs to his home with a story that "no one can beat," the presence of an adult with whom he can share the story is assumed. If the author is the implied narrator of Marco's tale, Marco's mother is his invisible adult audience. When Geisel was growing up, the parent who held the place of the missing interlocutor was Henrietta Seuss Geisel. Geisel was not simply reflecting the values of the German community when he chose his mother's maiden name as the surname of his storytelling persona.

In a 1983 interview the writer Jonathan Cott asked Geisel if his father would have approved of Marco's imaginative powers. "My mother would have loved it," he replied. "My father would have been critical."[11] He elaborated on his mother's attitude toward his work in a letter that he wrote to Robert Sullivan for a *Dartmouth Alumni Magazine* story: "My mother over-indulged me and seemed to be saying, 'Everything you do is great, just go ahead and do it.' "[12] It is Mother Seuss who enjoys hearing what this child narrator cannot say to Father Geisel. That this maternal figure is absent from Marco's story constitutes a dimension of its pathos.

Geisel recollected the language games he played with his mother as the most pleasurable of his childhood memories. Nettie was a gifted singer, and Ted often fell asleep to the sound of her singing the lyrics with which she advertised the pies she sold in her father's bakery: "Apple, mince, lemon . . . peach, apricot, pineapple . . . blueberry coconut, custard, and SQUASH!"[13] At bedtime she recited German poetry to Ted and read stories in German from the Brothers Grimm. Geisel later recalled the lines from Goethe's "The Erl-King" as a lasting inspiration: "Wer reitet so spaet durch Nacht und Wind? / Es ist ser Vater mit seinem Kind" ("Who rides so late through the windy night? / The father holding his young son so tight").[14] The poem is a father's conversation with his dying son as he feverishly rides though the wood to outrun death; it prefigures the dialogue between Marco and his father in *Mulberry Street*. Ted delighted in having Nettie sound out the rhymes of the verses she recited over and over. He also singled out the Brownies, imaginary creatures invented by the illustrator Palmer Cox in *The Brownies: Their Book*, as one of his childhood favorites: "I loved the Brownies—they were wonderful little creatures; in fact, they probably wakened my desire to draw."[15]

Nettie fostered the pleasure Ted took in the music of words when she presented him with *Goops and How to Be Them* by Gelett Burgess as a childhood primer in etiquette: "Like little ships set out to sea, I push my spoon away from me."[16] Ted subsequently attested to the profound effect that his mother had on his art when he remarked, "More than anyone else [my mother was responsible] for the rhythms in which I write and the urgency with which I do it."[17]

When Ted was young, Nettie enjoyed taking him to the Springfield Zoo and encouraged his habit of drawing caricatures of the animals on his bedroom walls. Ted's older sister, Marnie, recalled that in every room "on the bare plaster, was a cartoon done by Ted."[18] The bilingual environment in which Ted grew up fostered his knack for making up nonsensical-sounding names for the fantastic creatures he drew on the walls. His scrawls of such unpronounccable names on his wall drawings of the zoo's menagerie made his mother and sister laugh.

The chief prototype for his animal drawings was a brown stuffed dog named Theophrastus that his mother gave him when he was an infant.[19] Like Linus's blanket in Charles Schulz's "Charlie Brown" comics, Theophrastus performed the work of what D. W. Winnicott has called a transitional object. Inhabiting the occult zone between psychic and external reality, Theophrastus inspired Ted to construct imaginary interactions with Nettie through the doodles he drew on her walls and the nonsense words he assigned to them. Ted's nighttime drawings furthered Theophrastus's transition work by empowering Ted to cross the boundary separating wakefulness from sleep. Up to the day of his death Ted kept Theophrastus near his drawing board as a reminder of his mother's unconditional affirmation of the doodles that he produced as a child.[20]

Geisel recollected certain Springfield places, names, and events as distinct sources of pleasure and a direct influence on his work. In a 1986 interview with the *Springfield Union* to mark the fiftieth anniversary of the composition of *And to Think That I Saw It on Mulberry Street* he explained, "My excitement about being a writer came out of this place right here."[21] The Springfield armory that bore a distinct resemblance to a German *Schloss* was next door to the house in which he was born. The names of certain Springfield families—Wickersham, McElligot, McGrew, McGurk, and Terwilliger—and friends like Norval Bacon played significant parts in his imaginative life. He remembered the teetotaling Bumps and Haynes and the dentist Dr. Stebbins, whose patients came to his home.[22] When he was young the family would travel to the lake to gather blocks of ice to keep the beer cold throughout the summer. He recalled building sand castles and clamming at the family's beach house in Clinton, Connecticut.

When Ted was in grade school, T. R. and Nettie ordered Marnie, who was two years older, to hold her brother's hand when they came to busy intersections. But he often contrived excuses to lag behind Marnie so that he could take in the details of the panorama of commotion caused by the barking dogs chasing after children on their bicycles, the procession of horse-drawn vehicles—unwieldy ice wagons leaking torrents of water from their tailgates; grocers' delivery vans laden with crates of lettuce, corn, and rhubarb; black and gold carriages packed with barrels proudly advertising the Geisel family's trademark beer—flanked on one side by trolley cars rattling along their tracks and on the other by Hudson Sixes and bright red Indian motorcycles, all making their way along the cobblestone streets. The mobility of this scene said that Springfield was going places, and Ted felt he was at the center of it.

The contraptions Ted found in his father's workshop also provided valuable materials for his inventive imagination. He took particular delight in playing with his father's biceps-strengthening machine, the spring-clip top designed to keep flies away from spigots of beer barrels, and something he later described as the "silk-stocking back seam wrong detector mirror." One of the first books that he enjoyed reading turned his father's gift for marksmanship into its primary script. Peter Newell's *The Hole Book* had a hole punched through every page (each hole representing a gun shot). When he came to the lines "Tom Potts was fooling with a gun / (Such follies should not be), / When bang! The pesky thing went off / Most unexpectedly!" he began to understand how much fun reading could be.[23]

Ted's relationship with his parents turned on their differing reactions to his art. Like Nettie, his father liked to take him on tours of the zoo. But unlike Nettie, T. R. criticized his son's animal drawings for their mismatched and exaggerated features. Nettie's refusal to allow his father to erase the doodles that Ted had drawn on his bedroom walls constituted the first adult confirmation of the value of his artwork.

What Is This Little Boy Doing Here?

One aspect of Marco's story recalled Ted's fondest boyhood memories; another put him in touch with his family's deepest anxieties. The sources of that anxiety can be glimpsed by recalling the sights—the signs of the Geisel family brewery and of a supportive German American community—that are missing from Marco's story. Their absence reveals what distinguishes Marco from the boy who had lived through the disastrous consequences of these losses.

When Ted was Marco's age, Mulberry Street thronged with evidence of the Geisel family's prosperity. Barrels of beer from the Kalmbach and Geisel Brewing Company were distributed each day to a variety of shops and businesses along Mulberry Street. Employees carefully placed row upon row of wooden barrels of beer into the bed of a handsomely painted black carriage with gold trim and then hitched the carriage to a run of Clydesdale horses, whose bearing endowed the delivery rounds with an aura of Old World nobility. After returning home from school each day, Ted could not wait to greet his father as he stepped off the trolley that brought him home from the office.[24]

Before Ted reached his tenth birthday the Geisels suffered a dramatic change in status, from being representatives of Springfield's growing prosperity to targets of anti-German sentiment. In the period preceding the outbreak of World War I Springfielders turned against the German immigrant community. Books in German began to disappear from Springfield libraries; the Springfield Symphony stopped playing music by German composers. The rising tide of anti-German sentiment caused the U.S. Congress to repeal the charter of the two-million-member National German-American Alliance.[25] Congressmen recommended that sauerkraut be renamed "liberty cabbage" and that frankfurters be called "hot dogs."

Ted was subjected to verbal abuse and threats of physical violence as he traveled to and from school each day. Schoolmates yelled, "Hun!," "Drunken Kaiser!," or, more ominously, "Kill the Kaiser's Kid!" as they threw rocks and brickbats at him and Rex, his Boston bulldog. His sister Marnie developed agoraphobia out of the fear of being accosted on the street by hostile neighbors.

T. R. instructed his children in how to cope with their neighbors' hostility.[26]

Any pretense of neutrality disappeared on April 6, 1917, when German submarines began torpedoing American ships. Realizing that the United States would enter the war, Ted took part in a campaign to sell U.S. Liberty Bonds to demonstrate his family's patriotism. But going from door to door along Mulberry Street selling bonds soon became the basis for one of the most haunting events of his life.

After his paternal grandfather purchased $1,000 in war bonds as proof of the family's loyalty, Ted's total sales placed him among the top ten of the town's young salesmen. On May 2, 1918, the Geisels and the Seusses joined an audience of thousands to witness a ceremony at which former president Theodore Roosevelt would honor their fourteen-year-old's patriotism by awarding him a medal. Roosevelt went down the line congratulating each of the young men, repeating a laudatory statement praising each boy's accomplishment and pinning a medal on the honoree's chest. As he conferred one medal after another upon these deserving recipients, each presentation was met with thunderous applause. However, by the time he arrived at the spot on the stage where Ted was standing, Roosevelt had run out of medals. Lacking a medal to pin on Ted's lapel, Roosevelt bellowed, "What's this little boy doing here?" at the scoutmaster, who hurriedly shuffled Ted off the stage.[27]

At fourteen Ted's self-image was a precarious fusion of doubt and pride in his accomplishments. That evening the status of the entire family was to have been reaffirmed by Roosevelt, perhaps the nation's most prestigious public figure. But instead of his recognition as a Somebody who mattered, he was made into a Nobody, a pair of empty pants whisked off the stage.

The repetition of honorific phrases, such as the one Roosevelt used in presenting these medals, would later become a signature feature of Dr. Seuss's art of storytelling. Nonetheless the disgrace he experienced on that May evening left an emotional scar that stayed with Ted throughout the remainder of his life. He had no memory of stage fright before that event; after it, every invitation to appear on stage gave rise to an immobilizing fear that he articulated with a question that echoed Roosevelt's: "What am I doing here?"[28]

The public humiliation by a former president of the United States, whether intentional or not, reflected the devastating change in his family's status between 1914 and 1920. World War I ruined their social standing, and Prohibition deprived them of their primary source of income. Geisel's memories of his childhood would later oscillate between the privileged security that came from his paternal grandfather's status in Springfield society and the anxiety he experienced as the target of anti-German prejudice. The loss of his family's honor was subsequently inseparable from this quasi-ceremonial scene of public degradation.

However much the Geisels suffered before and during World War I, the prominence that they enjoyed during the first ten years of Ted's life did not entirely disintegrate until Congress voted the Eighteenth Amendment into law on January 16, 1919. Prohibition tore apart the fabric of the Geisel family. Before the law was enacted T. R. had become general manager and president of the family business. After Prohibition closed the doors of the Springfield Brewing Company, Ted reported, his father retreated to his room for six years, where Ted frequently overheard him "saying SOB, SOB over and over."[29]

When he entered Central High School in 1917 in the aftermath of his public humiliation, Ted went about devising strategies to recover his position. He retreated behind a series of masks to cope with the disintegration of his German American identity. Adopting theatrical personae put him in touch with who he wanted to be: a performer who deserved the respect of an admiring audience. The feeling that he was a pretender would remain with him for the rest of his life.

A year and a half ahead of his grade, he discovered he could get Bs in all of his classes without working. He ducked out of Latin to go to the movies and worked nights as an usher at Court Square Theater. He wrote one-liners known as grinds ("It'll be just our luck to be in Latin class when they turn back the clocks") for the weekly newspaper.[30] Ted joined the Mandolin Club, and he played Andrew Aguecheek in *Twelfth Night*. In his senior year he performed in blackface in a minstrel show called *Chicopee Surprised* that he wrote, staged, and directed. He was the joke and grind editor for the yearbook the *Pnalka*, and the class voted him class artist and class wit.[31]

At Central High he was encouraged to develop his writing talent by Edwin ("Red") Smith, who had recently graduated from Dartmouth College. Geisel later cited the rhymed *Beast Books* of Hilaire Belloc to which Red Smith had introduced him as a lasting inspiration for his children's books. Belloc's animals were always doing inappropriate things that were celebrated in captivating rhymes: "As a friend to the children commend me the Yak / You will find it exactly the thing / It will carry and fetch, you can ride on its back / or lead it about with a string." In his

Cautionary Tales Belloc described a girl named Matilda whose imagination may have been a prototype for Marco's:

Matilda told such Dreadful Lies.
It made one Gasp and Stretch one's Eyes:
Her Aunt, who, from her Earliest Youth,
Had kept a Strict Regard for Truth,
Attempted to Believe Matilda:
The effort very nearly killed her.[32]

At Central, Ted devised the dual personae of artist and clown to turn the negative stereotypes imposed upon the Geisels into empowering roles. He found satire and caricature particularly valuable in gaining mastery over the ridicule and derision. The dramatic oscillations in his social position inspired him to create two of his earliest pseudonyms. He signed the weekly column he wrote for the *Record* "Ole the Optimist" if its content was upbeat and "Pete the Pessimist" if it was not. The shift in his identity from Pete the Pessimist to Ole the Optimist also gave him access to the self-division through which he acknowledged his ambivalent feelings about a variety of social questions.

Later Geisel remembered his boyhood experiences in Springfield as significant sources for his stories, though he was less interested in recovering these traumatizing memories than in moving beyond them in children's books that conserved yet also transformed them. In reflecting on the influence of his boyhood on his later books, Geisel's biographer Charles Cohen described *And to Think That I Saw It on Mulberry Street* as a book "for children written by an adult, but [it was] created by someone who has not lost his memory of the fantasies and injustices of childhood. Their magic lies in Ted's ability to honestly address the injustices while ameliorating them with the sense of wonder established by the fantasies."[33] The book renewed the relationship between Ted and his father through what is subtracted from Marco's story. The sights that are missing from Marco's story reveal the effect the Volstead Act had on the Geisels.[34] Marco's unbeatable story replaces T. R.'s competitive drive (to continue running his business) with a form of creativity that cannot be taken away from him.

Marco's story is the fulfillment of a wish for a story that no one can beat. In seeing that which the father prohibits, Marco communicates with this unseen paternal aspect by recomposing T. R.'s suppressed competitive drive in the form of an unbeatable story. But he cannot communicate with his father's unacknowledged need to recover his self-worth without defying his command.

The means by which Geisel transcended his father's prohibition are discernible in the title he assigned to Marco's story. *And to Think That I Saw It on Mulberry Street* introduces a crucial qualification that changes Marco's relationship to the father's prohibition against fantasizing. The phrase "to think" invites readers to share in Marco's sense of wonder at the same time that it encourages them to make believe that Marco saw these events take place.

The depictions of the extravagant street scenes endow them with a reality all their own. The art of the tale inheres in the humor that it draws out of Marco's repeated reporting of what he wants to see in place of dutifully supplying the accurate version his father demands. Each time Marco compulsively returns to his father's restriction, he neither learns a lesson nor obeys the command. The comedy of *Mulberry Street* turns on Marco's inability to learn, or rather, his having to unlearn the same thing over and over again.

Read from this perspective, Marco's story represents a child's practical joke. It is Marco's way of taking in his father by letting him think that his son has in fact seen nothing but an ordinary horse-drawn wagon. Readers get in on the joke by enjoying the rollicking spectacle at the expense of the father's inability to make believe with Marco. Nonetheless Marco does not disobey his father so much as sidestep him by turning the order—"Keep your eyelids up and see what you can see"—into an injunction he follows to the letter. Marco provides evidence of his ability to keep his eyes open by bringing the animals that he has imagined into alignment with the vehicles that are most appropriate to them. Displaying his fidelity to visual precision, he decides to replace the horse pulling the canopied wagon with a zebra. Then, upon judging the zebra ill-suited to the task he has assigned it, he offers still more evidence of his commitment to observational accuracy: such a marvelous beast "With a cart that's so tame. / The story would really be better to hear / If the driver I saw were a charioteer." The inherent musicality and uptake in these lines both express and catalyze movement. The pictorial momentum of the story turns on Marco's lining up each new source of "horsepower"—beginning with the zebra and concluding with the elephant flanked by a team of giraffes—with the conveyance he deems appropriate to it. His father's regulation thereby supplies the energy for the unfolding of these increasingly animated street scenes. The final scene of *Mulberry Street* distinguishes those who can believe in the imaginary world—Marco's implied readers—from those who share his father's preference for matters of fact.

Charles Cohen delineated the effect of Ted's life on Dr. Seuss's art with this observation: "The prejudice directed at him in school during World War I, despite the respect his German family garnered in the community and the pride they took in their heritage, caused Ted to develop a hatred of such inequitable treatment."[35] Liberation from what traumatized him inspired the invention of characters who could act out and thereby work through what remained of his memories of the shame and humiliation that came from Prohibition and nativists' xenophobic stereotypes. Dr. Seuss's later children's books transformed his Springfield childhood into a Real Never-Never Land, a place in which Prohibition *never will have* happened and in which anti-German sentiments *never will have* exposed the Geisels to the derision of the Springfield townspeople. Each of these "nevers" was a gift from Dr. Seuss to his boyhood past.[36]

Two

BECOMING DR. SEUSS

THE PUBLICATION OF *AND TO THINK THAT I SAW IT ON MULBERRY Street* in the fall of 1937 marked a turning point in Geisel's artistic career. During the previous ten years he had published work in more than sixty different periodicals and more than a thousand newspapers,[1] but this was his first successful solo foray into the children's book market. The book critics for the *New York Times* and *Atlantic Monthly* wrote enthusiastic reviews, praising the author for his masterful understanding and spontaneous rendering of a child's mind. Clifton Fadiman singled it out for special tribute in a *New Yorker* book column: "They say it's for children, but better get a copy for yourself and marvel at the good Dr. Seuss's impossible pictures and the moral tale of the little boy who exaggerated not wisely but well."[2] Beatrix Potter was even more effusive, saying, "I think it the cleverest book I have met with for many years. The swing and merriment of the pictures, and the natural truthful simplicity of the untruthfulness."[3]

Heartened by the critics' favorable response, Geisel felt this breakthrough might change the shape of his career.[4]

He had had a lot of trouble getting the book published. Publishers were understandably wary of taking a chance in a Depression market on a children's book by someone who had established his reputation writing political satire for an adult readership. Perhaps because it provided an instance of the creative luck in which he needed to believe, Geisel repeatedly retold the story of the circumstances leading to the publication of his first children's book—like Marco, embellishing with each re-telling. Several versions of the story are in print. They differ significantly in the number of publishers—Geisel recalls as few as twenty and as many as forty-three—who rejected the manuscript.[5] Those publishers complained that the book either ignored or flouted the defining conventions of children's books. They believed that fantasy set to verse was not marketable and that the story's lack of a moral made it offensive. Geisel became increasingly combative in the face of these rejections. He defended the book against the charge of fantasy by describing what Marco saw on Mulberry Street as an accurate representation of the circus parades of his childhood, and he invoked the verse rhymes of Hilaire Belloc as a precedent for his own. But the criticism that "no moral or message" could be found in the book truly angered him.[6]

Geisel did finally succeed in finding a publisher when he accidentally ran into Mike McClintock, a former Dartmouth classmate, who earlier that day had been made editor of juvenile books at Vanguard Press. Unlike its previous readers, McClintock admired the book, and he immediately agreed to publish it. Vanguard printed fifteen thousand copies and took out a full-page ad in the August 28, 1937, *Publishers Weekly* exhorting booksellers, "Hitch on! This is the start of a parade that will take you places!" In recognition of the fact that he had found in McClintock the receptive adult interlocutor missing from Marco's story, Geisel changed the name of the book's child protagonist to Marco, which was the name of McClintock's son.[7] He also dedicated the book to McClintock's wife, "Helene McC, Mother of the One and Original Marco." In identifying his protagonist with the son of a former classmate, Geisel simply strengthened the Dartmouth family ties that had formed fifteen years earlier.

The Dartmouth Family

The alternative family Ted found at Dartmouth originated in Red Smith's class at Central High School. Smith regaled his students with wondrous accounts of his alma mater. Geisel suggested, "The reason so many kids went to Dartmouth at that particular time from the Springfield high school was probably Red Smith—a real stimulating guy who probably was responsible for my starting to write."[8]

When Ted took the train to Hanover, New Hampshire, in 1921 he was accompanied by sixteen other members of Red Smith's "gang." Over the next seventy years the bonds of fellowship he cultivated with Dartmouth classmates supplied him with the emotional resources of security, support, and acknowledgment. The members of the class of 1925 were singular in their loyalty to the college as well as to one another. Ted's Dartmouth classmates would become lifelong friends, a reliable audience for his art, honorary siblings, and the role models against whom he measured his own ambitions. He would also depend on them to get through difficult moments in his career and, as in Mike McClintock's case, help get his work published.[9]

In 1921 Dartmouth was looking to diversify its student body, and Geisel represented one of the students President Hopkins sought to realize this goal. At registration he listed his father's profession as brewer, "temporarily retired."[10] This joke covered over Ted's mortification at the family's loss of income. To offset the tuition fee of two hundred fifty dollars T. R. had to sell one of his father's real estate holdings.

Ted cherished the profound sense of community he found at Dartmouth. He even expressed grudging admiration for the hazing ceremonies in which upperclassmen initiated his class. The watering trough where seniors dunked pea-green freshmen when they caught them sitting on the senior fence afforded him special delight, as did the picture-book white buildings in Dartmouth Row. The turrets of the Rollins Chapel reminded him of the Springfield Armory. During his four years at Dartmouth Ted became a member of various campus organizations; in addition to Sigma Phi Epsilon fraternity he was a member of the Pleiades literary society and the Casque and Gauntlet Senior Society, a contributor to the *Aegis* and *The Dartmouth*, and the editor of the *Jack-O-Lantern*, the college humor magazine. It was Ted's work on the *Jack-O-Lantern* that defined his Dartmouth experience.

After meeting Norman Maclean in the winter of his freshman year, Ted began to hang out near the magazine's offices. Maclean, who later became a professor of English at the University of Chicago and the author of *A River Runs through It*, promoted Ted's work at the magazine, affording him the ideal space he needed to refine his skills. In the 1920s the *Jack-O-Lantern* was sold in newsstands in New York and Boston. Its chief competitors included the *Harvard Lampoon*, where Robert Benchley and Robert Sherwood were featured writers; the *Yale Record*, to which Cole Porter regularly contributed; the *Columbia Jester*, whose staff included Bennett Cerf; and the *Brown Jug*, which had S. J. Perelman.[11]

An English major, Ted valued his professors most for the lives they'd lived prior to taking up their teaching roles. One had been raised in Shanghai; another had lived on a ranch in California and taken a freighter to Brazil. His professor William Stewart's reminiscences of his trips to Paris, Leipzig, and Berlin made Ted eager to travel the world. But he dismissed most of the instruction he received in their courses for "teaching . . . the mechanics of getting water out of a well that may not exist."[12] The one exception was Ben Pressey, whose creative writing class played as important a role in Ted's college career as Smith had at Central. Pressey's were the only creative writing classes he ever attended. In one of the papers he wrote for the class he tried to prove that subject matter was not as important as method by writing a book review of the Boston & Maine train schedule.

The *Jack-O-Lantern* office usurped the classroom as the space in which he received the most valuable writing instruction. Ted shared the desire to write Great Literature "with a capital G and a capital L" with Norman Maclean, who had completed a novel in his senior year.[13] Both Ted and Maclean believed that writing for the magazine constituted the best apprenticeship in the craft. His other colleagues at the *Jack-O-Lantern* respected Ted for his inexhaustible creativity as well as his hard work. They frequently found him asleep in the magazine office with his head facedown on the typewriter. Geisel later said, "That's where I developed my general style and attitude, which has carried over—just to have fun and poke fun at things. It's a matter of satire. That's how we satirize a great many members of the human race and a great many other things that go on in the human race."[14]

At the *Jack-O-Lantern* Ted defined his reality in terms of his artistic commitments, and he created the persona with which he made good on those commitments. He discovered how to place Dartmouth's setting, characters, and events into a comic drama in which he took center stage. The staff collaborated in his illusion that the world was to be given over to play, and their enthusiastic responses to his performances encouraged his play-acting. With the *Jack-O-Lantern*'s readership as his audience, Ted cultivated the grand entrance, the surprise event, the decisive turn of phrase. His classmate Ken Montgomery described Ted's performance as a form of magic: "There was no sense of self-importance about him. But when he walked into a room it was like a magician's act. Birds flew out of his hands, and endless bright scarves and fireworks. Everything became brighter, happier, funnier. And he didn't try. Everything he did seemed to be a surprise, even to him."[15]

The Fatted Calf

Such performances required that he cultivate his talents as a cartoonist, satirist, and gag writer. One of the earliest of his published illustrations depicted a bulbous leg under a fashionably hemmed dress: "I got fascinated in college by Voltaire's and Swift's quest for truth via the use of outrageous (but controlled) exaggeration. So I wrote a few Swifts and Voltaires myself."[16] His drawing style was distinctive for its rococo

He Studied Under Webster

effects, which mirrored his flamboyant prose.[17] He made the college's most revered exemplars the targets of his satire. He poked fun at the prep school boys, who pretended to know everything, and the clubbers from Dartmouth's Outing Club, who spent all their time in the woods. He took particular delight in spoofing literary and political icons. In one cartoon not even the highly venerated Daniel Webster escaped his ridicule.

But Ted did not restrict himself to poking fun at cultural icons. He had been denied a fraternity bid during his freshman year because the brothers thought he was Jewish. "With my black hair and long nose, I was supposed to be Jewish. It took a year and a half before word got around that I wasn't."[18] The cost of disabusing them of this belief and winning acceptance was the construction of another cartoon, depicting a newly engaged Jewish couple marked by the features that had motivated Dartmouth's fraternities to exclude Ted from their fellowship. The rumors disappeared after he published the cartoon, and Ted pledged Sigma Phi Epsilon fraternity in his sophomore year. Nonetheless he continued using

"Nice Cohen"

Highball Thompson wins from Kid Sambo by a shade.

GERMAN MADE EASY

(Or, Who Stole the Schmierkas?)

Kaiser Friedrich (who is out drumming up votes for LaFollette)—Hans, mein Freund, wer war die Dame die ich mit Ihnen gestern Abend sah?

Hans (his niece, taken completely unawares)—Ach, Papa, die war keine Dame. Sie war meine Frau.

racist humor, for instance in a depiction of the winner of the fight between Kid Sambo and Highball Thompson as either a shade lighter or a shade darker. But no ethnic group was spared lampooning in Ted's contributions to the *Jack-O-Lantern*.

In his junior year he brought to life a menagerie of fantasized creatures, some of which would serve as an arsenal for the "Boids and Beasties" columns he subsequently created at *Judge* magazine. But the primary topics of his humor were Prohibition, sex, and gin. "All you had to do was say 'gin' and people would laugh," he said in a later interview.[19]

The popularity of Ted's work resulted in his being recognized as one of Dartmouth's most influential students. His circle of friends included the brightest of Dartmouth's men of letters. In addition to Maclean, this coterie consisted of Alexander Laing, Donald Bartlett, and Whitney Campbell. Each of these men played key roles in fostering Ted's career after his graduation. Laing, who also worked at the *Jack-O-Lantern*, became a staff writer for the *New Yorker* before returning to Dartmouth as a

Tucked in Tight

professor of English. Bartlett, who graduated in 1924, would later share a year with Ted at Oxford as a Rhodes Scholar. Perhaps the most significant of Ted's friendships at Dartmouth was with Campbell. Ted considered Whit Campbell, who later gained national prominence in the field of corporate law, the most scholarly and challenging of his peers.

In their junior year Ted told Campbell that he would consider his college career a failure were he not elected the editor of *Jack-O-Lantern*. Campbell, in turn, divulged his desire to become the editor of *The Dartmouth*. Having shared their deepest aspirations, the two men became allies in 'the campaign to realize them. On May 15, 1924, the *Jack-O-Lantern* board elected Ted its editor in chief; that same month Campbell was selected editor of *The Dartmouth*. Geisel later memorialized the date in one of his books: May 15 is the date on which Horton is successful in his effort to save the village of Whoville from certain destruction.[20]

After graduating Geisel frequently returned to campus for class reunions and to judge the Dartmouth winter carnival contest, in which students built snow sculptures that were often modeled after his own "beasties." Ted himself had constructed a snow sculpture similar to the "Alabastard" on the porch of Phi Gamma Delta fraternity during the 1930 competition. He named Horton after his classmate Horton Conrad; he dedicated *Yertle the Turtle and Other Stories* to Donald Bartlett; he named the Wah Hoo River from *I Had Trouble in Getting to Solla Sollew* after the Dartmouth cheer (Wah-Hoo-Wah); and he placed the name of the *Jack-O-Lantern* staffer Curtis Abel on a signpost pointing to Salina, Kansas (Abel's hometown) in *I Can Read with My Eyes Shut!* Geisel also wrote advertisements supporting the Dartmouth Fund and together with his wife founded the Ted and Helen Geisel Third Century Professorship (of which I was a beneficiary in 1990).

Following the success of the Dr. Seuss books, Geisel was the subject of numerous columns and interviews in *The Dartmouth*, and he was frequently featured in adulatory articles in the *Dartmouth Alumni Magazine*, which took an uncommon interest in his success. His murals and paintings were displayed periodically in the college's art galleries and at the Hood Museum. In 1955 Dartmouth awarded him the first of his eight honorary doctorates. At his fiftieth class reunion in 1975 his career was the subject of seventeen display cases in Baker Library.[21] In every way the familial affections between Geisel and Dartmouth were mutual, steady, and long-lasting.

The Invention of Seuss

The fellowships Ted forged at Dartmouth provided for his sense of belonging from 1921 until the outbreak of World War II. The letters he wrote to Maclean, Campbell, and Robert Sharp during the summers he spent at his family home in Springfield were filled with plans for the upcoming year—where to live and what projects to take up upon his return to campus.[22] His sister Marnie was a supportive link between his family in Springfield and his extended family in Hanover. After he was elected to the *Jack-O-Lantern* staff in 1923 he invited Marnie to attend the Dartmouth Winter Carnival. She was met at the railroad station by a horse-drawn sleigh that delivered her to rounds of ice-skating at Occom Pond, and she received a rush from Ted's brothers at Sigma Phi Epsilon fraternity. Having met Ted's circle of friends she was able to commiserate with him during the summer months when he was away from campus.

The year 1925, Ted's last year of college, began auspiciously: he took over editorial responsibilities for the *Jack-O-Lantern* and enjoyed the social standing that came with the position. The year before, he had been one of twenty students elected a member of the Casque and Gauntlet, perhaps the most prestigious of the senior honor societies. Campbell, along with Pete Blodgett, Larry Leavitt, and Kenneth Montgomery, initiated him into the renowned Knights of the Round Table, and fifteen of the twenty members moved into the Casque and Gauntlet's house during their senior year. But Ted decided to share a more economical room with Robert Sharp in a clapboard boardinghouse for students and faculty that was run by Ma and Pa Randall.

As graduation approached Ted was surrounded by classmates who had clear plans for their future. Campbell was about to enter Harvard Law School, Blodgett prepared for a career in banking, and Sharp was going to graduate school in English. At a final meeting of the Casque and Gauntlet the members voted their predictions for one another. After the ballots were counted the Knights of the Round Table achieved unanimity on only one decision: that Ted was "least likely to succeed."[23] With a grade point average of 2.45 and an academic ranking of 133 in a class of 387, the vote did not come as a complete surprise. He turned the incident into an occasion to demonstrate his gifts at self-caricature. Having succeeded in becoming the *Jack-O-Lantern*'s editor, Ted had acquired the only honor that truly mattered to him.

But he was about to undergo an experience that proved almost as disorienting as his family's misfortunes in Springfield. On the evening of Holy Saturday, April 13, 1925, Ted invited nine members of the magazine's staff to his room at the Randall house, where they partook of the bottle of gin he had purchased that day from a bootlegger who had earned President Hopkins's seal of approval. At the peak of the evening's festivities, Ted and Curtis Abel climbed onto the tin roof of the house and squirted seltzer water at each other. Ignorant of the source of the fluids showering down from his roof (and deficient of the capacity for merriment), Pa Randall imagined the worst of offenses and called the Hanover police. When the chief of police raided the apartment, he took all the young men into custody for violation of the liquor laws.

After a hearing Craven Laycock, the redoubtable dean of students, placed Ted and his friends on probation for defying Prohibition on one of the holiest days in the Christian calendar. Furthermore Laycock removed Ted from the position of editor of the *Jack-O-Lantern* and barred him from contributing to the periodical he'd spent four years establishing as a cutting-edge college publication. Ted considered the terms of the punishment excessively severe. Laycock's decision to remove him from the editorship of the *Jack-O-Lantern* recalled previous scenes of humiliation that he had undergone: his schoolmates' insults during World War I, Roosevelt's public shaming, the family's loss of its livelihood. Without his title as editor of the *Jack-O-Lantern*, Ted felt as if part of his identity was missing.

Ted expected his father, who had been comparably wronged by the injustice of Prohibition, to mount a campaign protesting the harshness of the dean's decision. To his son's disappointment, however, T. R. wrote in complete support of the terms of Dean Laycock's punishment: "You have violated the rules and you have been penalized, consequently abide by the decision of the authorities. And in this connection, Ted, I want you to serve your full sentence conscientiously. . . . Make an attempt the next few weeks to eradicate this blot from your good record."[24]

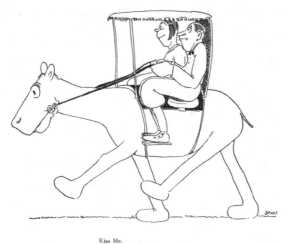

Kiss Me.
Whaddaya think this is—a taxi?

Ted obeyed the conditions of the dean's punishment; he removed his name from the masthead and stopped publishing materials under his given name. Within the week, however, he submitted a series of cartoons that were published under sundry pseudonyms, among them the horticulturalist L. Burbank, the biochemist L. Pasteur, and the decadent poet Dante Gabriel Rossetti. Finally he turned to his own middle name and for the first time signed "Seuss" under a cartoon.

He had followed the letter but overturned the intent of the dean's justice. By subtracting the patronymic from his surname, Ted had quite literally followed his father's demand that he wipe the blot from his record. "Seuss" differed from his other pseudonyms in that it neither concealed nor obliterated his identity. Initially it may have provided the guise needed to continue publishing his cartoons, but more significantly it created an extension of Ted by which he was able to liberate and realize his art.

"Seuss" turned the dean's punishment into a prohibition that Ted enjoyed transgressing. What began as an act of rebellion became one of self-expression. Not privy to what the *Jack-O-Lantern* staffers and Ted's inner circle knew all too well, the dean was turned into the dupe of one of his comic performances. The signature enabled Ted to transform his shame and indignation into pleasure by literally making a name for himself. "Seuss" was at once a password into the world of make-believe to which Nettie had introduced him in his childhood and an incitement to recover its magic.

It was poetic justice. Geisel from Springfield became Seuss at Dartmouth because of an incident at Dartmouth that recalled traumatizing experiences in Springfield. His punishment stemmed from a violation of the same law that had ruined the family business. His banishment from the *Jack-O-Lantern* echoed his previous humiliation at the hands of President Roosevelt.

"To what extent this corny subterfuge fooled the dean, I never found out," he mused fifty years later. "But that's how 'Seuss' first came to be used, as my signature."[25] Whether or not it technically worked, it liberated Ted from constraints that otherwise would have silenced him. But he would not comprehend the full significance of the signature until he linked the persona with the author of his children's books.

OXFORD INTERLUDE

Ted graduated from Dartmouth on June 23, 1925. But he still had one more Dartmouth adventure (or misadventure) to undergo. It began when his father asked what he intended to do after graduation. True to his penchant for exaggeration, Ted responded that he would be attending Oxford on a Campbell Fellowship from Dartmouth. Although he had in fact only applied for the fellowship, Ted's father was so overjoyed at this news that he went across the street to report it to the editor of the *Springfield Union*, Maurice Sherman, himself a Dartmouth man, who printed the story as fact.[26]

When Ted mustered the courage to explain the disparity between the printed story and the fact that the Oxford fellowship would not be forthcoming, T. R. decided that he had to turn his son's exaggeration into the truth and sold some inherited real estate to send him to Oxford. Ted sailed for England on the MS *Cedric* on August 25, 1925, and soon took up a room at Lincoln College.

Ted never liked Oxford. He loathed its pretentiousness and class snobbery; he disliked the tasteless English food, and he detested the dining rituals. Although he was a college graduate, as a first-year Oxford man he was required to sit at the freshman table, where he was four years older than his tablemates. The prevailing social ethos at Oxford after the war supplied his British classmates with two grounds for excluding him from their clubs: his German ancestry and his American sense of humor. They considered the former an affront to British patriotism and the latter an insult to English respectability. Ted spent most of his time with other American exiles he met there. For recreation he played tennis regularly with Donald Bartlett, who was now at Exeter.

Measured against his stated ambition to become a professor of literature, his year at Oxford can only be described as a failure. But Bartlett and his expatriate companions encouraged him to think of his time spent there as a basis for a *Jack-O-Lantern* skit. Ted seized the opportunity. Donning the persona of the sophisticated satirist, he created skits and gags about his experiences at

Oxford in which he caricatured its least attractive traits: the pomposity, the snobbery, the cultivation of eccentricities that accentuated class distinctions. In one of these performances he explained that what finally prompted him to leave Oxford was Sir Oliver Onions's two-hour lecture on the punctuation of *King Lear*: "This don, Sir Oliver Onions, had dug up all of the old Shakespearean folios and lamented that some had more semicolons than commas. And some had more commas than periods.... I listened for a while and then went to my room and packed."[27] Ted's Dartmouth entourage concurred with his conviction that he was not cut out to be an English teacher.

Doodles in the margins of his notebook indicate where he preferred to locate his attention during lectures. During his class on Anglo-Saxon for beginners he drew a pair of baroque daggers in the margins. The page also features a coat of arms with a central panel from which a bird tries to extricate itself. On a page of notes on Keats's odes, he tracked three dogs moving in terror across a high wire strung across terrain populated by a chicken wearing a windmill for a tail. His response to Emile Legouis's lecture on Wordsworth and Jonathan Swift best summarizes his attitude toward his Oxford classes: it is a sketch of himself sinking into dark waters with the caption "Mr. Legouis attempts once more to attract my attention in a lecture entitled ... ?"[28]

In a year otherwise given over to slapstick comedy, however, Ted did meet someone at Oxford who significantly altered the direction of his life. Marian Helen Palmer was a Wellesley graduate six years older than Ted. She attended some of the same classes and would stare over his shoulder at the doodles he drew. During their class on Anglo-Saxon she watched as he drew angel wings on a cow with a sagging udder and ram's horns. "You're crazy to be a professor," she declared. "What you really want to do is draw. . . . That's a very fine flying cow!"[29] Helen was the first person to propose that he bring these figures from the margins into the center of his artistic project. Her evaluation may have resonated with his mother's confirmation of his artistic talents, but her pronouncing it at Oxford possessed all the force of a vocational calling.

The couple spent more time together than Oxford rules allowed. Helen quickly became Ted's intimate confidante and a lively addition to the expatriate group he organized. She played the role in his adult life that his mother had played during his childhood: an attendant spirit who enabled him to trust in his gifts. Over the next forty years she was the primary inspiration for his artwork, the only critic whose opinion he trusted, and an indispensable collaborator on his children's books. An inextricable dimension of his creative imagination, Helen was as necessary to it as his past.

Ted's Dartmouth family welcomed Helen into its fellowship; the Geisels, who thought their engagement impulsive, took longer to welcome her into their family.

Dr. Seuss and the Roaring Twenties

In February 1927 Geisel returned to his childhood home after ten months of traveling through Europe and began to bombard publishers with samples of his work. In April of that year he brought his portfolio to the Dartmouth Club to have lunch with a group of friends who had already launched their careers in New York. "I have tramped all over this bloody town," he wrote to Campbell, "and been tossed out of Boni and Liveright, Harcourt Brace, Paramount Pictures, Metro-Goldwyn, three advertising agencies, *Life*, *Judge*, and three public conveniences. My results are this: One picture 'taken' by *Life* to 'consider more carefully.' One order for half a dozen grocery store cartoons for *Al Brown's Journal*. One appointment with [Alexander] Laing this afternoon. We are going to go into business together insofar as *The New Yorker* magazine is concerned. He has been accepted there and I am consciously cultivating him. Keryst! What is this world coming to?"[30]

Drawing on his time abroad Geisel pitched a series of cartoons on *Eminent Europeans*—the croupier, the palace guide, the quack in the baptistery in Pisa—to *Life* magazine. But he did not succeed in getting them published. He got his first break on July 16, 1927, when the *Saturday Evening Post* published a cartoon of two upper-class British female tourists perched atop the backs of two camels led by an Arab guide in blackface. The caption reads, "I Am So Thrilled, My Dear! At Last I Can Understand The Ecstasy Lawrence Experienced When He Raced Posthaste Across The Sands of Arabia in Pursuit of the Fleeting Arab." The

cartoon was signed "Seuss."[31] Immediately after he was paid for the cartoon Geisel moved from Springfield to New York.

His first apartment was a walk-up studio in Greenwich Village that he shared with John C. Rose, who had worked on the *Jack-O-Lantern*. Rose knew someone who sold advertising for *Judge* and helped Geisel get cartoons published there as well. He later remembered, "I wasn't getting anywhere at all, until John suddenly said one day, 'There's a guy called "Beef Vernon," of my class at Dartmouth, who has just landed a job as a salesman to sell advertising for *Judge*. His job won't last long, because nobody buys any advertising in *Judge*. But maybe, before Beef gets fired, we can con him into introducing you to Norman Anthony, the editor.' "[32]

Geisel's first *Judge* cartoon, which appeared on October 22, 1927, was signed "Seuss." Within weeks, he added "Dr." to his signature. The honorific supplied him with symbolic compensation for the doctorate he never received at Oxford.

In his work for *Judge*, which was comparable to *The New Yorker* in its layout and appeal, Geisel refined and extended his repertoire of comic techniques, though Dartmouth and his former classmates continued to play featured roles in many of his early

DISSATISFIED WIFE—*And to think that today I could have been the wife of a six-day bike racer—if I hadn't listened to your rot about Higher Art!*

cartoons. In one of these he portrayed Campbell using his pet elephant's trunk as an ashtray. Another cartoon pictured the fraternity initiation of Paul Jerman; he had to hunt a fifty-foot whale with a hatpin. Cornelius Kurtz, a student who had bunked in the room across from him in Topliff Hall, was shown using his pet snake to reserve a subway seat. Thomas Phelps Carpenter, who was a member of the Casque and Gauntlet, was pictured crossbreeding a dachshund with a reindeer.[33]

As these examples indicate, Geisel's early usages of "Dr. Seuss" associated the signature with a series of comic performances that drew on routines concocted at the *Jack-O-Lantern*. In a letter to Campbell he explained that he was saving his personal identity for the Great American Novel he intended to write after he found his bearings in the world of letters.[34] He had already tried his hand at writing such a work during his trek through Europe following the Oxford fiasco. Upon failing to persuade any publisher of the merits of his two-volume masterwork, however, Geisel characteristically turned this personal defeat into the occasion for comic pleasure: "When it wouldn't sell, I condensed it into one volume. When that wouldn't sell, I boiled it down into a long short story. Next I cut it to a short, short story. Finally, I sold it as a two-line gag. Now I can't even remember the gag."[35]

The majority of Geisel's early satires, parodies, and slapstick routines revolved around alcohol. They all cast Dr. Seuss in the role of comic antagonist of the organized hypocrisy of Prohibition. He also introduced a cartoon series entitled "Being Ye Inside Dope on King Arthur's Court."[36] After the Knights of the Round Table ordered Sir Galahad to stay behind and banish alcohol, King Arthur commissioned Merlin to construct an illicit still in his cellar. He introduced an elephant as a heroic boozer in a satire entitled

"Quaffling with the Pachyderms OR Why I Prefer the West Side Speak-easies."[37] He drew a pileup of teetering turtles in a spoof on how to drink eggnog.[38] These subjects remained a staple of Geisel's cartoons and became the basis for his reputation.

Geisel's first sustained artistic production was a *Judge* column entitled "Boids and Beasties." Another early favorite was "Goah's Ark." The title references a wild menagerie of creatures that emanated from hallucinations Noah's dissolute brother Goah saw while in the throes of alcohol withdrawal. It was signed "Dr. Theophrastus Seuss." But the totemic creature who presided over this bestiary was an imaginary animal he called a Hippocrass; the word is a variant of the name of the oldest alcoholic drink. His drawings of the Hippocrass depicted a gangly, two-legged animal with wings, floppy ears, and a smile. In the script that accompanied these drawings Geisel described the Hippocrass as a nightmare that entered into the real world by escaping from a hallucination brought on by delirium tremens.[39]

In one of the published versions of this real nightmare, Geisel represented the Hippocrass as the embodiment of anti-Prohibition joviality, which had to be imprisoned upon its arrival on Ellis Island. President Coolidge, who enforced Prohibition, was depicted in a sombrero branded with a swastika. But Mayor James Walker, an opponent of Prohibition, rescued the Hippocrass and gave him the key to the city. Once free the Hippocrass championed the free spirit of the roaring twenties.[40]

Following its illicit union with another of Geisel's Beasties, the Hippocrass produced a hybrid offspring called a Blinx, who inspired the following lines about the formidable Grandmother Squeers:

> Granny Squeers has a hound-sort of a beast called a
> Blinx.
> You don't call him by whistling; you merely take drinks,
> And when he appears we just get up astride
> And he takes us right out for a heavenly ride.
> We cling to his back just as long as we're able,
> Then he gently deposits us under the table.[41]

In an effort to advertise the comic appeal of his signature persona, Geisel and his Dartmouth friends became regulars at the famous New York speakeasies, where Geisel impersonated Dr. Seuss's most popular routines. His after-hours pranks in the speakeasies, and the murals that he painted on the walls of the most famous of them, gave Geisel a certain notoriety. His devotees in *College Humor* took to publishing parodies of his work under the signature "Dr. Souse."[42]

Geisel soon felt secure enough in his reputation to propose to Helen. But T. R insisted that they delay the wedding until after

Marnie gave birth to her first child, Peggy Dahmen. Ted and Helen married on November 29, 1927, twenty-eight days after Peggy's birthday. The newlyweds moved into a walkup in the Lower East Side, which was so dangerous a neighborhood that Geisel traveled to work each day carrying a cane loaded with a spring blade. "Helen and I worked harder than ever to get out of this place," he later recalled.[43]

Flit Years

Geisel's first real break was the result of an accident similar to his encounter with Mike McClintock. The cartoon that attracted mighty Standard Oil of New Jersey, the makers of Flit bug spray, portrayed a drunken knight sprawled across his bed with his armor on and a menacing-looking dragon hovering above him. The caption read, "Darn it all, another Dragon. And just after I'd sprayed the whole castle with Flit!"[44] According to Geisel, he had

Mediæval Tenant—*Darn it all, another Dragon. And just after I'd sprayed the whole castle with Flit!*

flipped a coin to decide whether to use Flit or the name of the rival bug spray, Fly-Tox. The cartoon came to the attention of the Flit Products Division of Standard Oil when Grace (Mrs. Lincoln) Cheaves, the wife of the advertising executive who handled the Flit account, saw the cartoon while flipping through the pages of *Judge* at a hairdresser's salon. She urged her husband to get Geisel on Standard Oil's payroll.[45]

The cartoon led to a contract and a series of advertisements organized around the catchphrase "Quick, Henry, the Flit!" which quickly became part of American popular culture. A song was written around it, and such notable comedians as Fred Allen and Jack Benny used it as a dependable punch line in their radio skits. Flit sales increased enough for Standard Oil to pay Geisel twelve thousand dollars a year. He composed Flit ads for portions of nine years from May 31, 1928, to August 22, 1938, returned in 1940 and 1941, and very likely would have continued producing them indefinitely had Harry Truman not accused Standard Oil of making treasonous deals with Nazi Germany in March 1942.[46]

The Flit contract provided Geisel's career with a secure economic base. But he still derived the strongest sense of self-worth from the recognition his performances received from a live Dartmouth audience. The Knight who had been voted least likely to succeed was now earning more money than the most successful of his Dartmouth classmates. Eager to put his newfound celebrity on display, he traveled to Hanover in the spring of 1928 to meet former classmates and professors at his reunion and to attend commencement ceremonies. Upon returning to New York, Ted and Helen moved into a spacious apartment on West End Avenue.

The celebrity associated with his work for Flit made his cartoons and comic skits much sought after. In addition to his contributions to *Judge*, *Life* magazine and *Liberty* paid him three hundred dollars per page for the parodies and drawings he sent them. *Vanity Fair* offered him even more. The Geisels continued their upward trajectory by moving yet again, to 17 East Ninety-sixth Street, where their lavish dinner parties and his practical jokes became the talk of the town. Friends who were invited to dine at the Geisels' residence reported that it was not unusual to find wealthy business executives seated alongside Broadway actors and Peruvian polo players at the couple's table.[47]

When Geisel arrived for a black-tie dinner party thrown by Frank A. Vanderlip, the president of National City Bank and a member of New York's power elite, he contrived an excuse to survey his host's kitchen. Upon gaining entry he inserted a dime-store pearl inside an oyster that was later served to the head of a Wall Street brokerage firm. When he discovered the pearl, the Wall Street mogul engaged his host and hostess in a heated argument over who had legal rights to the treasure. Geisel left it to Helen to explain the joke.[48]

Over the next eight years he spent time hobnobbing with the wealthy on Long Island, traveled to more than thirty countries in Europe, the Middle East, and South America, and moved again, this time to the northwest corner of Ninety-second Street and Park Avenue. He also advertised expeditions to nonexistent places under the auspices of Seuss Travel Bureau; organized a fake detective agency called Surely, Goodness, and Mercy ("We'll follow you the rest of your life"); produced a new menagerie of beasties with names like the Carbo-nockus and the Raspo-nockus to advertise Esso automobile lubricants; sculpted beasties out of animal horns his father sent from the Springfield Zoo; completed a five-foot-square oil painting of *The Rape of the Sabine Woman*; started the Hejji comics series for the Hearst syndicate; and in 1935, as Admiral Seuss, launched the Seuss Navy with Esso Marine, into which he inducted more "phony Farraguts" than Kentucky turned out colonels.[49]

When Nettie died in 1931, her loss opened a void that neither Dr. Seuss's humor nor Geisel's successful career could fill. To take his mind off her death, Geisel made his first foray into the world of children's books by accepting an invitation from Viking Press to illustrate a collection of schoolboy howlers—"Adolescence is the stage between puberty and adultery," "Acrimony, sometimes called holy, is another name for marriage"—called *Boners*.[50] His drawings were well received, and *Boners* went through four printings in two months. He produced illustrations for another volume of *Boners* that same year. Elated by the response to his artwork, Dr. Seuss wrote and illustrated an ABC book of strange animals addressed to children. But the color required to reproduce his pictures would have resulted in a volume priced at $150.00. After Viking, Simon & Schuster, and Bobbs-Merrill turned the book down as too costly to be marketed during the Depression, the librarian at Dartmouth invited him to display it in the school's art gallery.[51]

In addition to bolstering Geisel's ego, the recognition he continued to receive from his alma mater encouraged him to treat his career with comedic theatrics. He frequently met reporters in his pajamas, told them he never worked before three in the afternoon, and swore to maintain this line of work as long as he could.[52] He was especially fond of posing as the mock hero of a lifelong tragicomic struggle against humiliation. As his twenty-ninth birthday approached he planted the rumor that Dr. Seuss was an armless man who drew with his toes. Geisel's self-deprecating attitude toward his career betrayed an insecurity that his lucrative contract with Flit could not alleviate. His self-mockery effected a contradictory relationship to his career: it enabled him to identify with the accomplishments that he simultaneously derided. A product of the satiric fantasies that he created, Geisel was in part the real thing and in part its parody.

In moving an audience to laugh at his prosperous career, Geisel attempted to release himself from responsibility for its success or failure. The double vision that he cultivated through this self-mockery derived from the fact that the success of his early writings depended in large part on targeting the Prohibition laws that had ruined the family business. After Prohibition came to an end in 1933, he lost his comic foil. He began producing commercials for the beverages Prohibition had banned. He composed ads for Schaefer Brewery and the American Can Company, invented "Chief Gansett" logos for the Narragansett Brewing Company, and created the Hankey Bird for Hankey Bannister Scotch.[53]

Despite his spectacular success in advertising, Geisel felt there was something missing from his life. His friends and Dartmouth classmates who were making far less money had nevertheless established themselves in more respectable professions. His mother's death and the fact that Germany was once again playing the bully in Europe left him feeling adrift in high seas that not even the admiral in chief of the Seuss Navy could navigate.

Germany's belligerent posturing brought back anxious memories of World War I. *And to Think That I Saw It on Mulberry Street* began his coming to terms with these memories. Children's books were ranked relatively low in the hierarchy of literary genres, but Geisel, in the midst of a career without bearings, found himself gravitating toward them. When Vanguard Press published his second children's book, *The 500 Hats of Bartholomew Cubbins,* in November 1938 the book received praise comparable to that of *Mulberry Street. Booklist* described it as composed of the best features of the Sunday comics and the fairy tale and praised it as a "lovely piece of tomfoolery which keeps up the suspense and surprise until the last page."[54] However, its sales were deflated because its forty-eight pages required Vanguard to price *The 500 Hats of Bartholomew Cubbins* at $1.50.

Dr. Seuss's second children's book addressed the criticism directed against *And to Think That I Saw It on Mulberry Street.* Rather than a verse account of a child's serial exaggerations, Dr. Seuss wrote a story in prose with a moral and a recognizable story line. Whereas the first book reads like a cumulative nursery rhyme, this book is a folkloric fantasy with a happy ending. Like *The Emperor's Clothes, The 500 Hats of Bartholomew Cubbins* turns on a plot device that renders a monarch dependent on a child for the legitimation of his rule.

Bartholomew Cubbins and King Derwin occupy opposite extremes of the Kingdom of Didd. From the top of his castle King Derwin can take in the entire kingdom: "It was a mighty view and made King Derwin feel very important." Bartholomew saw the exact same view but "saw it backward." The king's mighty view "made Bartholomew Cubbins feel mighty small." Despite his lowly position Bartholomew stops King Derwin's parade in its tracks when, after removing his hat, Bartholomew uncovers another—and another, and another. King Derwin demands, "Do you or do you *not* take off your hat before the King?"[55]

Bartholomew wants to show due deference to the king, but his hats will not comply. The king demands that Bartholomew remove his hat because his authority is founded upon this public sign of respect. Removing one's hat is not merely a gesture of obedience to King Derwin; doing so produces the social recognition of the king's power. The fact that Bartholomew cannot remove his hat endows him with a power that in a sense exceeds the king's.

Given the threat the boy poses to his sovereignty, King Derwin feels compelled to order Bartholomew marched to the top of the castle's turret and thrown to his death. As Bartholomew walks up the stairs one of the king's advisors, Sir Alaric, the keeper of the records, notices that the boy's hats are beginning to change in shape. The closer Bartholomew gets to the top, the fancier his hats become. His five-hundredth hat "had a ruby larger than any the King himself had ever owned. It had ostrich plumes, and cockatoo plumes, and mockingbird plumes, and paradise plumes. Beside *such* a hat even the King's Crown seemed like nothing."

The story's conclusion reveals that the king's sovereign power—which King Derwin exercises in the death sentence he pronounces upon Bartholomew—does not exceed but depends upon the hat that appears on Bartholomew's head just before he is to be thrown to his death. The king's desire to purchase the hat as the insignia of his royal authority shows how the person of the king and Bartholomew's hat have become more or less equivalent signs of sovereign power.

The review of the book that Geisel most valued was written for the *Dartmouth Alumni Magazine* by his classmate Alexander Laing, who was then teaching English at Dartmouth: "His several other occupations, madly fascinating as they are, may have been only preludes to a discovery of his proper vocation. That he is a rare and loopy genius has been common knowledge from an early epoch of his undergrad troubles. It now becomes plain that his is the self-consistent, happy madness beloved by children. I do not see what is to prevent him from becoming the Grimm of our times."[56] Professor Laing punctuated his favorable appraisal of Geisel's writings with a helpful Seussian rhyme:

> You're wrong as the deuce
> And you shouldn't rejoice
> If you're calling him Seuss
> He pronounces it Soice.[57]

Geisel was even more gratified by the college librarian's request to keep the original manuscript in the Baker Library's archive. He wrote, "[The solicitation] comes as a thrill to a bloke who can't make up his mind whether he's an author or just a lowly advertising man."[58]

Geisel may have thought that he was moving up a notch in the literary hierarchy, but in moving from Marco's Mulberry Street to Bartholomew's Kingdom of Didd he was in fact moving from his actual Springfield past to an artificial literary past. In *The 500 Hats of Bartholomew Cubbins* Dr. Seuss sacrificed Marco's remarkable make-believe world to a prosaic allegory designed to illustrate the injustices of monarchy. In writing this fairy tale and the next, *The King's Stilts* (1939), he followed the dictates of the critics of *And to Think That I Saw It on Mulberry Street*. Rather than writing a verse fantasy without a message, he wrote two traditional fairy tales in prose with strong messages.

Whereas the *The 500 Hats of Bartholomew Cubbins* was a revision of *The Emperor's Clothes*, Dr. Seuss's next children's book, *The King's Stilts*, conveyed an anti-Prohibition message cloaked in a modern fairy tale. When his young page Eric helps King Birtram recover his stilts from the place where the wicked Lord Droon has hidden them, the child's discovery affirms the story's message that all work and no play can demoralize a monarchy. Eric's recovery of the king's stilts adds the element of childlike merrymaking whose absence from the adult world poses a threat to that world's survival. If the king can't get wobbly on his stilts at night, he cannot stand upright and rule during the day.

In both fairy tales Dr. Seuss's art advances the political empowerment of children. The king's stilts and Bartholomew's hats represent children's playthings that cannot be fully integrated within the already existing order and that thereby radically challenge the order of things. Dr. Seuss was no longer reconstructing Ted's boyhood experience; in these prose fables he was teaching moral lessons. Geisel's democratic impulses and his liberal humanitarianism are evident in both works. But these fairy tales are most interesting for the light they throw on the successful verse fantasy that preceded them and on the masterpieces that would follow.

Geisel and his wife celebrated the launch of *The 500 Hats of Bartholomew Cubbins* on their eleventh wedding anniversary, November 29, 1938, by dedicating it to an imaginary child they named "Chrysanthemum-Pearl, aged 89 months, going on 90." Their invention of Chrysanthemum-Pearl enabled the couple to come to terms with the ovarectomy Helen had undergone in the fourth year of their marriage that made it impossible for her to have children.

At this time they were also mulling over a tempting offer of more money and better publicity if Geisel left Vanguard for Random House. After he signed the contract offered by Random House's publisher, Bennett Cerf, Ted started work on an adult fairytale about seven Lady Godivas and their relationships with the seven Peeping Brothers (Tom Peeping was the eldest of the Peeping boys). *The Seven Lady Godivas* bore the subtitle *The True Facts Concerning History's Barest Family*.

But Dr. Seuss's first book under Cerf's auspices was a critical and commercial failure. Of the ten thousand copies that Random House printed, only twenty-five hundred were sold in 1939;

during the first six months of 1940 sales totaled twenty-three copies.[59] The 1939 sales of *The King's Stilts*, the first of Dr. Seuss's children's books published by Random House, were even more disappointing. Despite the tour that Cerf had arranged to promote it, only 4,684 copies of the book were sold in 1939, and in 1940 only 394 copies were sold. Furthermore it took two years before *Mulberry Street* went into a second printing of six thousand copies.

The paltry royalties he received from the sale of his books could not possibly support the lifestyle to which the Geisels had become accustomed. But Geisel was about to go through a series of events that would lead him to dissociate from the worlds of advertising and adult satire and devote his signature persona exclusively to the writing of children's books.

Three

Dr. Seuss Returns

At a dinner ceremony held during Dartmouth's 1940 reunion, Helen turned to Dorothy Leavitt and remarked, "I'm very upset because Ted has that elephant up a tree and he doesn't know how he's going to get him down." She went on to explain that she and Ted had come to this turn in the plot of a children's book called *Horton Hatches the Egg*. Leavitt later attested, "That's not the sort of conversation you forget!"[1]

According to Geisel, the elephant got up the tree by accident. He described sitting in a chair next to an open window in his studio one day when a sudden gust of wind blew one transparent sketch atop another. The result was the image of an elephant sitting in a tree. "What is an elephant doing in a tree?" he asked himself. "Obviously hatching an egg. But how did the egg get there? Hmmm . . . a bird must have left it. Where did the bird go?"[2]

Horton Hatches the Egg, which Random House published in 1940, recounts the trials of an elephant named Horton who fulfills a promise made to a bird named Maysie to sit on her egg, even after she has abandoned it, because "an elephant's faithful—one hundred per cent." Horton's fidelity to the maxim that an elephant is unswervingly true to his word almost causes him to lose his freedom.

Dr. Seuss, however, found it difficult to remain faithful to the narrative that he hatched. "I keep losing my story line and Helen has to find it again," he reported.[3] It was Helen who finally discovered the way to bring the elephant down from the tree. She bridged the plot in a way that rendered the story's conclusion—the emergence from the egg of a winged elephant bird—a biological necessity. Her pivotal contribution included the book's climactic lines:

> "My goodness! My *gracious*!" they shouted. "MY WORD!
> *It's something brand new!*
> IT'S AN ELEPHANT BIRD!!"[4]

F. Scott Fitzgerald articulates one of the core fantasies of the roaring twenties in *The Great Gatsby* when he describes Jay Gatsby as having given birth to the platonic conception of himself. Horton undergoes a comparable rebirth when he recognizes himself as the origin of the winged creature that hatches out of the egg he has nurtured. Horton is regenerated out of the constancy of his word. The story of the winged creature who was hatched by such an improbable parent could also be construed as an allegory of Geisel's own creative life, to which he was delivered by Helen's declaration, "That's a very fine flying cow!"

GEISEL GOES TO WAR

On the night of June 14, 1940, while Nazi tanks were rolling into Paris, Geisel listened to his radio and heard Senator Gerald P. Nye of North Dakota, perhaps the nation's foremost isolationist, urge the United States to stay out of the war. Geisel remembered, "I found that I could no longer keep my mind on drawing pictures of Horton the Elephant."[5] He put Horton's story aside for several months in favor of drawing political cartoons. After he showed one that caricatured Mussolini's chief propagandist, Virginia Gayda, to his friend Zinny Vanderlip, she sent it to Ralph Ingersoll, who had resigned from a lucrative job at *Time* magazine to found the Popular Front newspaper *PM*. Ingersoll published Geisel's cartoon in the January 30, 1941, issue. Over the next two years he would publish many more.

The end of Prohibition liberated Geisel from one of the psychic fixations, the loss of the family's business, to which his humor had been bound. But he had not yet exorcised the traces of resentment he continued to harbor over the anti-German sentiments directed against the Geisels at the outset of World War I. His trip to Germany in 1936 had awakened painful memories of the family's persecution, and Hitler's occupation of Paris in 1940 inspired him to take command of the stereotypes to which American nativists had reduced him and his family.

An April 1941 Gallup poll reported that 80 percent of Americans were strongly opposed to any involvement in the war with Germany. Geisel dedicated his *PM* cartoons to the task of overcoming his readers' isolationism, though he did not restrict the targets of the cartoons to Nazi Germany and fascist Italy. A June 1941 cartoon depicts an American eagle reclining in an easy chair

Said a bird in the midst of a Blitz,
"Up to now they've scored very few hitz,
So I'll sit on my canny
Old Star Spangled Fanny . . ."
And on it he sitz and he sitz.

By Dr. Seuss

with bombs exploding all around it.[6] Another cartoon of the same time represents Nazis and America Firsters as Siamese twins.[7] Similarly disdainful caricatures of American nativists animated many of the satires he composed for *PM*. The vast majority of his cartoons directed his anger and political invective against the two social formations— German authoritarianism and American nativism—he considered responsible for creating the hostile environment of his Springfield childhood.

Especially excoriating were his caricatures of American fascists like Father Coughlin and Senator Nye, and of German Americans who sympathized with Germany's bellicosity such as Charles Lindbergh. One of Geisel's earliest *PM* cartoons imprinted a horse's ass on Senator Nye. But it was his skewering of Lindbergh that finally prompted Ingersoll to ask him to supply between three and five editorial cartoons a week. Geisel wrote the following lines describing the famous pilot:

The Lone Eagle had flown
The Atlantic alone
With fortitude and a ham sandwich.
Great courage that took.
But he shivered and shook
At the sound of the gruff German landgwich.[8]

Lindbergh, who was honored by the German government in 1938, exhorted the United States to remain neutral. Geisel found the example Lindbergh set extraordinarily deplorable because he feared that Lindbergh's Nazi loyalties would cast suspicion on all German Americans.

Geisel devoted his attacks on Lindbergh to the destruction of all traces of German Americans' sympathetic associations with Nazi Germany. But his grand obsession was with Adolf Hitler. He drew a series of caricatures entitled "Mein Kampf," one of which showed Hitler refusing a bottle of milk because it came from Jewish-sounding Holstein cows. He also abhorred French Premier Pierre Laval for his collaboration with Hitler. Geisel's cartoons became famous when Nelson Rockefeller, in his office as the coordinator of Inter-American Affairs, used Geisel's *PM* cartoons to promote inter-American cooperation.

The *PM* cartoons were signed "Dr. Seuss," but it was Geisel's very real rage that was emotionally responsible for their creation. The haunting specter of "Kill the Kaiser's Kid!" spurred him on. He harnessed all the tools—invective, satire, parody, and caricature—he had cultivated while writing for *Judge* to the skills he had refined in advertising Flit under his Dr. Seuss pseudonym.

Horton Hatches the Egg, completed with Helen's help, sold 5,801 copies in 1940; its sales fell to 1,645 the following year.

Bennett Cerf nevertheless gave him an additional advance against its future royalties. With this five hundred dollars, the Geisels had enough money to invest in a vacation home in La Jolla, California. They bought a hillside lot overlooking the La Jolla Beach and Tennis Club and built a small ranch house surrounded by farm gates and olive trees. They moved in June 1941, and Geisel began mailing his cartoons to New York City. It would take another seven years before he rededicated himself to the writing of children's books.

In his cartoon of Pearl Harbor that was published on December 8, 1941, Geisel drew an enormous black explosion, "WAR!," that sent a Seussian bird labeled "Isolationism" reeling across the sky with the caption "He Never Knew What Hit Him!"[9] After Pearl Harbor American authorities seized the MS *Kungsholm* for the transport of troops. On the same day that the government refitted the *Kungsholm* for wartime service *PM* published the first of Geisel's cartoons promoting the purchase of defense savings bonds and stamps to raise money for the military effort.

The annual subsidy Ingersoll received from the investment banker Marshall Field III meant that *PM* was free from obligations to advertisers and could thus be an ideologically independent magazine. In his 1940 prospectus Ingersoll summarized the magazine's purpose in the following declarations: "We are against people who push other people around, in this country or abroad. We propose to crusade for those who seek constructively to improve the way men live together."[10] Geisel was even more succinct. "*PM* was against people who pushed people around," he said. Then he added, "I liked that."[11]

In addition to articles expressing opposition to Nazism and fascism, Max Lerner and I. F. Stone wrote regular columns addressing labor demands, civil rights, and women's emancipation. Lerner described the staff's collective project in terms of a single antagonism: "The common ground we had was Adolf Hitler and Franklin Roosevelt, one the serpent to be slain, the other to slay him."[12] Geisel was proud of joining men and women he respected, among them Lerner, Stone, Lillian Hellman, Kenneth Crawford, and Zinny Vanderlip, in the campaign against racism and anti-Semitism.

News of the horrors to which Jewish populations had been subjected led Geisel to regret the anti-Semitism depicted in some of his earlier artwork. He metaphorically severed himself from this collective prejudice with a cartoon published in the April 2, 1942, issue of *PM* that showed American Nazis struggling to convince Uncle Sam to permit an executioner named "Anti-Semitism" to cut off both his hands.[13]

Geisel also endorsed *PM*'s antisegregationist politics in the South as well as its efforts to promote workers' rights. He weighed

in on the issue of the rights of black laborers by demanding that they be given a larger share of employment in defense industries. In late April 1942 he drew a cartoon representing a Boss of Industry standing atop a huge tank pulling two miniaturized tanks depicted as segregated by "Discriminating Employer." The first of these tanks, which trailed far behind the Boss's vehicle, was operated by a figure designated "Jewish Labor." "Negro Labor" lagged even farther behind.[14]

The *New Yorker* magazine dismissed *PM*'s staff as a bunch of "young fogeys," Geisel later recalled. "But I think we were, rather, a bunch of honest but slightly cockeyed crusaders. . . . Whatever I lacked . . . (and it was plenty) . . . as a polished practitioner of the subtle art of caricature, I did become prolifically proficient in venting my spleen."[15] Charles Cohen attributes one of the possible motives for Geisel's *PM* crusade against injustice to his experiencing "anti-German prejudice personally during World War I."[16] Regardless of his motivation, Geisel's involvement with *PM*

"Gimme some kerosene, some excelsior and a blow torch. Ma wants to bake a cake."

significantly expanded the reach of his political and social sympathies.

Despite his support of domestic minoritics, however, the nation's war against Japan resulted in cartoons that drew on racist stereotypes to which he was otherwise opposed. In October 1941 he drew a caricature of Hirohito kneeling next to Hitler behind an American eagle and whispering, "No . . . YOU'RE supposed to shove him over MY back."[17] In November 1941 he personified Japan as a saboteur in the guise of a shopper.[18] After Japanese submarines were reported just off the coast of southern California, the U.S. government ordered that nearly 120,000 Japanese American citizens be relocated to internment camps.

Fort Fox

In February 1942 *Newsweek* described Geisel's satire as "razor keen," and on May 27 his patriotic work was awarded a Civilian

Savings commendation. But his critics questioned the authenticity of his wartime journalism, claiming that he confined his battles to the editorial pages of *PM*. Though he was too old for the draft, Geisel volunteered to join the military in 1943 at the age of thirty-nine. He was assigned to the Information and Education Division, with a commission in Frank Capra's signal corps unit that was run out of a leased Hollywood studio and came to be known as Fort Fox.

When friends asked why he worked for the Hollywood Front, Geisel replied that he joined the unit to explain why Americans fight. Others who worked for the unit included enlisted men Irving Wallace, Carl Foreman, Gene Fleury, and P. D. Eastman. Among the unit's animators were Chuck Jones, Fritz Freleng, Bob Clampett, and Frank Tashlin. Fort Fox also boasted such notable writers as John Cheever, Irving Wallace, James Hilton, William Saroyan, Irwin Shaw, and Lillian Hellman; Ben Hecht, John Huston, and Julius and Philip Epstein were also in the unit. Many of the artists that Geisel worked alongside at Fort Fox had close ties with children's literature. Eric Knight was well known for *Lassie, Come Home*, and W. Munro Leaf had written *The Story of Ferdinand*. Phil Eastman, who would subsequently publish books in Dr. Seuss's Beginner Books series, was the author of *Are You My Mother?* Capra presented incoming recruits with the following description of Fort Fox's rationale: "You are working for a common cause. Your personal egos and idiosyncrasies are unimportant. There will be no personal credit for your work, either on the screen or in the press. The only press notices we are eager to read are those of American victories."[19]

Geisel turned his service at Fort Fox into an opportunity to learn the craft of filmmaking. The Capra unit produced biweekly newsreels for the armed services that included animated cartoons with training messages; these were shown from 1943 to 1945. While at Fort Fox Geisel worked diligently and built lifelong alliances with fellow artists. He credited Capra with teaching him the importance of conciseness. He learned even more about the juxtaposition of words and visual images from his coworkers in the animation studio.

At Fort Fox Geisel was part of a creative community that educated the public in the rationale for war. The fellowship he experienced with the artists there resembled the camaraderie he had enjoyed with the *Jack-O-Lantern* staff. The friendships that he developed in Capra's unit would prove comparably important in advancing his career. His fellow artists at Fort Fox soon supplanted the *Jack-O-Lantern* staff as the peer group with whose projects he compared his own. Rather than serving as an admiring audience for his self-mocking routines, these artists exemplified the social importance of artistic production and inspired him to become similarly committed. He began reevaluating the sources and aims of his own art.

Geisel's comrades admired his gift for using humor to sell things. He teamed up with Munro Leaf to produce shorts on the dangers posed to army trainees by the *Anopheles* mosquito. In the animated film *This Is Ann*, Geisel drew illustrations that portrayed the mosquito as a vamp who forsook whiskey, gin, beer, and rum and coke for "G.I. blood."[20] During his year and a half at Fort Fox he worked with Bob Clampett, who had done the animated version of *Horton Hatches the Egg* for Warner Brothers, and with Chuck Jones he helped produce thirty episodes of the animated cartoon *Private SNAFU*, an acronym that a voice-over translated euphemistically as "Situation Normal

All . . . FOULED . . . Up." He forged especially strong creative bonds with Jones, who later translated several of Dr. Seuss's children's books into popular animated films. One of Geisel's rhymed cartoons, *Gripes*, explored what would happen if Private SNAFU realized his fantasy of running the show; all pretense of discipline disappeared, and the men under his command chased girls and drank booze, leaving no troops on duty to defend against German attack. Geisel's collaborations with Jones won them a statuette, the Fort Fox version of the Oscar cast in the image of Private SNAFU.[21]

In March 1944 Geisel was promoted to the rank of major, and Capra entrusted him with the job of creating an occupation film dubbed Project 6010 that explained what the soldiers' jobs would be when Germany surrendered and American troops remained as an occupation force. The film is entitled *Your Job in Germany*. It begins with a voice-over warning, "Just as American soldiers had to do this job twenty-six years ago, so other American soldiers—your sons—might have to do it again another twenty-odd years from now."[22] The copy he wrote for the final script includes very strong language that at times fails to distinguish the nation's war with Nazi Germany from hostility directed against the entirety of the German people: "The Nazi Party may be gone, but Nazi thinking, Nazi training and Nazi trickery remains. The German lust for conquest is not dead. . . . You will not argue with them. You will not be friendly. . . . There must be no fraternization with any of the German people."[23] After the war Geisel was openly critical of the film's message: "I strongly believed in everything I wrote in this film with the exception of the Non-Fraternization conclusion . . . which I wrote as an officer acting under orders . . . and later worked to get rescinded."[24]

Following the liberation of Paris in 1944 the Allies drew up plans for the occupation of Germany. On November 11, 1944, Major Geisel was directed to take his top-secret film to Ireland, England, and Paris and ask the Army High Command to screen it. Generals Bradley, McSherry, and Eisenhower all approved of *Your Job in Germany*, but General Patton responded by yelling "Bullshit!" and storming out of the screening room.[25]

When Geisel traveled to Luxembourg in December 1944 he ran into his former *PM* editor, now Lieutenant Colonel Ingersoll, who sent him on a special mission to Bastogne. While he was stationed there the Germans started an offensive that left Geisel trapped ten miles behind the enemy's lines. Here's how Major Geisel, who swore that if he ever saw action, he'd grab his gun by the barrel and throw it, described what happened next:

> The thing that probably saved my life, was that I got there in the early morning and the Germans didn't arrive until that night. I found Bastogne pretty boring and . . . got on the other side of the line and got cut off. . . . With the aid of another MP who was also lost and hastening through a downpour in the opposite direction, we learned we were ten miles behind German lines. We were trapped three days before being rescued by the British. . . . The retreat we beat was accomplished with a speed that will never be beaten.[26]

MARNIE

On September 14, 1944, Geisel's beloved sister Marnie died in Springfield of coronary thrombosis at the age of forty-three. He was inconsolable. Marnie had first developed agoraphobia during childhood, which Geisel believed was a reaction to the public taunting they had endured as children. Her inability to recover led to an increasingly reclusive lifestyle. She also began to drink heavily. Her daughter, Peggy, wrote the following poignant account of an incident between Marnie and T. R.: "Mother was upset with me when I was about nine or ten, and Grampie went into the kitchen and said something to her to calm things . . . it was related to alcohol. . . . Then he walked out and did not speak to her again for four or five years, even though we kept living at the house. That's how he handled anger."[27]

Because the Geisels never traveled to Springfield during the five years of Marnie's estrangement from her father, she thought they had taken sides against her. Geisel, however, felt nothing but affection for his older sister. After their mother's death Marnie had supplied the affective connection to his childhood home, though they were unable to renew their relationship prior to her death. Marnie was buried near their mother in the family plot at Oak Grove Cemetery.

The Geisels subsequently invited Peggy, who was seventeen when her mother died, to move in with them. She had grown up in Geisel's childhood home, and when she moved into his tower studio in La Jolla her presence renewed Ted's emotional ties to Springfield.

Writing for the Boom: Rebel with a Cause

Marnie's death intensified Geisel's resolve to return home from World War II with the painful memories from World War I behind him. Like other *PM* contributors he was hopeful that the veterans' experience of "democratization" would keep alive the troops' efforts to transform U.S. society and "that the men who wore the uniform would return home changed by what they had experienced through working side by side with those from many other nations or Americans of different races and ethnic backgrounds."[28] In a 1944 memo he wrote, "Much of what we have gained is, at the moment of victory, threatened. . . . Racial tension within our Army threatens to grow. . . . Disillusionment, cynicism, distrust, bitterness, are already souring the milk of human kindness; maggots are already eating the fruits of victory."[29]

In producing the SNAFU shorts he learned how to combine instruction with entertainment. However, he felt that the propaganda he produced had failed to instill democratic principles in adults whose prejudices were already determined by education and upbringing. He worried in particular that his mode of addressing enlisted men had been too simple-minded: "Being remote from the soldier, we tend to talk down to the soldier when we should be talking *with* the soldier. His world is mud and we tend to talk to him from our world of clean sheets. The information we give him is the information he wants—and is greedy for—but we often irritate him by the way we present it."[30]

Despite these concerns Geisel had uncovered so many talents while producing his wartime work that he had difficulty deciding which ones to cultivate. His return home from war elicited anxieties that were even more troubling than those he experienced after returning from Oxford in 1927. He tried out several career paths that drew on different aspects of the creative persona he had developed over the preceding twenty years. In addition to writing articles for *Life* and monthly children's stories for *Redbook*, he submitted advertising concepts to Ford Motors, drew political cartoons for the *New Republic*, created film scripts, produced animated cartoons, and delivered lectures on children's literature.

Warner Brothers won an Oscar for its 1946 remake of *Your Job in Germany*, entitled *Hitler Lives*. That same year Jack Warner offered Geisel a contract for five hundred dollars per week to work on the script of *Rebel without a Cause*. The Geisels certainly needed the money. During the war Helen had written children's books for Disney and Golden Books—*Donald Duck Sees South America* and *Tommy's Wonderful Rides* were two of her most popular titles—that had supplied their primary source of income. By 1945 Geisel had learned to expect almost no income from his own children's books; the royalties from *Mulberry Street* and *Horton* came to only a few hundred dollars a year. Nonetheless not even the promise of a secure income could overcome his aversion to working with a committee of scriptwriters. Geisel resigned from Warner Studios after a few months with the explanation, "We'd rather make our own mistakes than have squads of people make them."[31]

His sojourn in advertising required Geisel to create desire for products. His job during the war had mandated that he invent reasons to dislike different groups of people, including his German ancestors. His cartoons attacking fascist structures were motivated by what remained of his indignation over childhood resentments. The more than four hundred political cartoons he published in *PM* had positioned Geisel to confront head-on the German authoritarianism that cast a long shadow over his youth.

Geisel may have succeeded in exorcising the specter of German authoritarianism left over from his boyhood, but the means whereby he had accomplished this catharsis sometimes left him feeling as though he were a reflection of the name-calling schoolmates who had inflicted the psychic wounds. His cartoons were uninformed by the wit and zany inventiveness of his *Judge* drawings, and they lacked the unconstrained fantasy of his children's books.

Ironically Geisel did not achieve artistic maturity until he discovered that the deep sources of his art lay sedimented in his Springfield experiences. The children's literature scholar Henry Jenkins has shrewdly observed that in the postwar years Geisel "saw children, rather than adults, as a more promising audience for these lessons." After World War II children composed the readership Geisel wanted to educate and be educated by. He sought this younger audience because he believed that political education "might more productively start at childhood."[32] He empathized with children's struggle against the corrupting influence of grown-up hatreds, and he trusted that writing children's books would enable him to better the world. In realizing this belief, Geisel connected the disparate manifestations of his immense creativity—the surreal images, nonsensical verse, boisterous rhythms, irreverent posturings, outrageous punning, slapstick humor, off rhymes—with the playfulness he knew as a child.

The postwar baby boom's dramatic enlargement of the market for children's books also strongly influenced Geisel's decision to rededicate himself to the genre. From the 1930s to the early 1940s the birth rate hovered near 2.5 million per year. In 1946 the number of births skyrocketed to 3.47 million and continued to rise throughout the 1950s, reaching a peak in 1953 of 4.3 million. It wasn't until 1964, the final year of the baby boom, that births fell back to 4 million. Able to imagine a much larger audience for his children's books, Geisel re-sorted his artistic commitments to address the educational needs of the boomer generation.

Logical Insanity

In 1949 Professor Brewster Ghiselin invited Geisel to join a group of distinguished writers and critics that included Vladimir Nabokov, Wallace Stegner, William Carlos Williams, and John Crowe Ransom at a ten-day writers' conference in Utah. Geisel gave public lectures and led six workshops on the genre and history of children's literature and its place in contemporary popular culture. During his lectures he articulated his desire to write a children's literature that was more than simply sugar-coated and condescending tales fostered by adult sentimentality. Geisel named this mentality "Mrs. Mulvaneyism." His lectures drew a strong contrast between Mrs. Mulvaneyism's stifling conventions and his own aspiration to write books that drew on the inventiveness of the comics children loved to read: "Over *here* we put our readers to sleep. Over *there*, they wake 'em up with action. . . . Over *here*, we bore them with grandpa's dull reminiscences of the past. Over *there*, they offer glimpses of the future."[33] Affirming the desire to combine popular entertainment with social uplift, he warned his audience of writers against becoming propagandists who were more interested in message than story. The ideal children's book would make reading both fun and meaningful.

Geisel devoted his seminars to the differences between contemporary children's books, fairy tales, and classical myths. He argued that children's interest in classical myths was restricted to the vivid images of its heroes and heroines. They liked Hermes' winged shoes, Thor's hammer, and Pandora's box, but moral lessons went right by them. He described Aesop's fables as too cold and abstract to hold a child's interests and singled out the humor of "Puss 'n Boots" as a felicitous turn in the history of fairy tales. He particularly liked the books of wit and realism written by Hans Christian Andersen, Robert Louis Stevenson, and Mark Twain.

Geisel described the best children's stories as those that addressed what he thought were children's seven basic needs: love, security, belonging, achievement, knowledge, change, aesthetics. "They want *fun*. They want *play*. They want *nonsense*." He added, "If you write with these needs in mind, you'll have a chance of having children accept you."[34]

He wanted to protect children from adults' stultifying control by giving them a sense of their own potential. He asked the adults in the audience to take seriously children's frustration with authoritarian rules and to respect children's innate sense of justice. Because children are "thwarted people," their chief "idea of tragedy is when someone says you can't do that."[35] He challenged would-be writers to avoid the racist stereotypes so common in children's literature and to foster a greater commitment to equality and justice. He also cautioned the writers against patronizing their readers. To respect the child's autonomy and intelligence, children's books should be understated rather than overtly preachy: "Children analyze fantasy. They know you're kidding them. There's got to be logic in the *way* you kid them. Their fun is pretending . . . making believe they believe it."[36] Geisel elaborated on the concept of plausible nonsense in an interview with Mary Lyden: "Children will grant you any premise, but after that—you've got to stay on the same key. You can't switch from A major to B-flat minor in the middle of the story. What I have tried to do is use implausible facts to create a plausible world—plausible—that is, from a child's point of view."[37] He called the method whereby he manipulated his universe to appear reasonable to an ever skeptical audience "logical insanity."[38]

The Utah workshop enabled Geisel to make good on his college years' desire to teach. But when he sent his lecture notes to Saxe Commins, his editor at Random House, Commins discouraged this ambition by pointing out that it would impede his creative work. Geisel's career dilemmas become obvious in the following account of the conversation: "He helped me realize that a paragraph in a children's book is equal to a chapter in an adult book. He convinced me that I had as much responsibility to take as much time and work as hard as [adult writers] did."[39]

Children's ability to reimagine the rules by which people live convinced Geisel that writing children's books might transform the cognitive structures behind political parties and social formations. He began to think of childhood as a quasi-utopian space in which belief in peace, social equality, and democratic participation could be reanimated. He also believed that children possess a sense of fairness and justice as well as a hunger to belong and to participate. When empowered to make their own choices in their own space, children can open up new possibilities. Furthermore, he insisted, children are immune to propaganda: "You can't pour didacticism down little throats."[40] The challenge was to protect children from the corruption of adults' overbearing power rather than indoctrinate them into any orthodoxy. Geisel later spelled out this philosophy in his essay "Writing for Children: A Mission": "In these days of tension and confusion, writers are beginning to realize that Books for Children have a greater potential for good, or evil, than any other form of literature on earth. They realize that the new generations *must* grow up to be more intelligent than *ours*."[41]

But Geisel's decision to focus his talents on creating children's books also led him to reevaluate his art. His 1952 essay on the sources of children's laughter articulates the terms of this reevaluation:

> You began to laugh at people your family feared or despised, people they felt inferior to, or people they felt better than. . . . Then you learned it was socially advantageous to laugh at Protestants and/or Catholics. You readily learned, according to your conditions, that you could become the bright boy of the party by harpooning a hook into the Jews (or Christians), labor (or capital), or the Turnverein or the Strawberry festival.
>
> You still laughed for fun, but the fun was getting hemmed in by a world of regulations. You were laughing at subjects according to their listing in the ledger.[42]

Children, he went on, unlike their adult counterparts, exaggerate for the sheer fun of it: "On their humor there is no political or social pressure gauge. That, I think, is why we maverick humorists prefer to write exclusively for children."[43]

In this essay Geisel was reflecting on the conditions of his own artistic imagination. His examination of the constraints that social prejudice had placed on his art made it clear that he was no longer working from the same mental framework that inspired his aggressive satires and caricatures. Presumably because of the prejudice he experienced as a German American child during World War I, his attitude toward minorities had been concocted out of an ambivalent mixture of tolerance and condescension.

In his adult satires, Geisel had targeted each of the ethnic groups mentioned in this passage (with the possible exception of the German community represented by the Turnverein) as the setup for his joke work. In the art he produced after the war he taught his readers to understand that people from all countries matter. Rather than joining fellow artists from Fort Fox such as Irving Wallace, Irwin Shaw, and Lillian Hellman, who went about refashioning their wartime art to meet the needs of the cold war, Geisel aspired to dissociate his art from a war mentality. He wanted to let go of the emotional baggage that had informed the aggressive satire of his wartime art. When he turned to children's literature, he renounced the artistic practices that sprang from such animosity. Seeing things from the child's perspective freed him from ingrained patterns of behavior and a compulsive creative stance.

When Geisel assumed the persona of the children's book writer as his primary identity he replaced invective, parody, and satire with children's verse fantasy as his primary genre. He endowed the other facets of his artistic personality with a composite perspective. To complete the transition from political cartoonist to children's book author, however, he also yoked the persona of Dr. Seuss to a new aesthetic structure.

Dr. Seuss's art originated from the need to elude an authoritarian censor. From the moment Geisel contrived his secret artistic persona at Dartmouth, Dr. Seuss deftly circumvented moral inhibitions and logical constraints. His postwar art transformed overcoming prohibitions from the major theme of his caricatures and satires into a defining structural feature of his books. The comic technique involved both getting past adult censors and retroactively including these adults in the events by which they were evaded. Dr. Seuss invented his own language to overcome the border separating sense from nonsense; he fabricated creatures that defied the boundary separating animals from humans; and he unfailingly crossed the line separating meaningful statements from the sheer fun of making logical nonsense.

The child narrator of *On Beyond Zebra!* states this more simply when he remarks: "In the places I go there are things that I see / That I never could spell if I stopped with the Z."[44]

THE OOBLECK AND THIDWICK

Dr. Seuss published eight children's books between 1947 and 1956. All of these books were part of the same postwar project. Three—*Thidwick the Big-Hearted Moose* (1948), *Bartholomew and the Oobleck* (1949), and *Horton Hears a Who* (1954)—make reference to war. Three others—*McElligot's Pool* (1947), *If I Ran the Zoo* (1950), and *If I Ran the Circus* (1956)—have explicit homecoming topics. Two of them—*Scrambled Eggs Super!* (1953) and *On Beyond Zebra!* (1955)—are organized around scenes of instruction.

Bartholomew and the Oobleck and *Thidwick the Big-Hearted Moose* rework the wartime realities of assault from the air and territorial occupation into backdrops for children's tales. *Bartholomew and the Oobleck* returns Dr. Seuss to the Kingdom of Didd, where Bartholomew had previously performed his hat tricks, only this time King Derwin makes matters much worse for his subjects by turning the focus for his megalomania on the heavens rather than Bartholomew's headgear.

The king brings destruction down upon his kingdom when he seeks to extend his rule over what falls from the sky. Bored with snow, fog, and rain, the king asks for something new. The heavens answer his request by letting a green substance called Oobleck ooze out of the firmament and all over the land of Didd.

Bartholomew had demonstrated the significance of the most lowly subject to the success of monarchical rule at the conclusion to *The 500 Hats of Bartholomew Cubbins*. Apparently bolstered by that lesson, a now hatless Bartholomew warns the king about the ecological dangers the Oobleck poses, but the king does nothing until Oobleck gums up the entire kingdom. The Oobleck doesn't stop dropping until Bartholomew issues the following rebuke to his king: "You may be a mighty king. But you're sitting in Oobleck up to your chin. And so is everyone else in your land. And you won't even say you're sorry. You're no sort of king at all."[45]

After King Derwin pronounces the simple words "I am sorry," his confession of public remorse changes the conditions of his rule. Rather than placing his imperial desires above the earthly life he shares with all of his subjects, the king addresses his "I am

sorry" to his subjects as well as to the landscape devastated by his command.

Thidwick the Big-Hearted Moose turns on the theme of occupation, and it too concludes with the changes made to an unjust government. The story begins when a menagerie of forest creatures decides to take up residence in the antlers of a moose named Thidwick, who feels duty-bound by the rules of hospitality to accommodate them:

> "This bird," murmured Thidwick, "is sort of a pest!
> But I'm a good sport, so I'll just let him rest,
> For a host, above all, must be nice to his guest."[46]

But the "pests" who have taken up residence in Thidwick's antlers not only exploit his hospitality, they physically abuse their host. For his part Thidwick remains obedient to the rule commanding a host to be hospitable to his guests, even after his guests take a vote elevating their needs above his survival. The story builds to a suspenseful moment of truth in which Thidwick must decide whether to cast out his guests and look to his own safety or continue to follow the rules and risk starving to death. With the following lines, Dr. Seuss communicates Thidwick's dilemma to the reader:

> Now what was the big-hearted moose going to do?
> Well what would YOU do
> If it happened to YOU?

The resolution of this drama is at once utterly appropriate and wholly unexpected: Thidwick sheds his antlers, thus separating from the part of himself that has been taken over by self-interested squatters. At the story's end Thidwick's insufferable

guests confront a much more malevolent form of selfishness: hunters who kill for sheer sport. Still perched on Thidwick's discarded antlers, the squatters end up stuffed and mounted on the wall of the Harvard Club.

These books address the imperial aggrandizement and unjust occupation that precipitated two world wars. Rather than narrating them from the perspective of the adults responsible for the wars, Dr. Seuss envisions such initiatives from a child's perspective. When Bartholomew reprimands the king in the name of "everyone else" in the kingdom affected by his command, he speaks from the standpoint of children who are the first to acknowledge remorse whenever they make a mess of things. Many children have also experienced frustration at the sight of their sandlot or playground being overtaken by uninvited guests, but like Thidwick they soon learn how to let go of what was never wholly their own. Unlike the human adults represented in these tales, Bartholomew and Thidwick adjudicate these matters with remedies that fall far short of war.

THE SPRINGFIELD CYCLE

Writing *Bartholomew and the Oobleck* and *Thidwick the Big-Hearted Moose* enabled Dr. Seuss to dissociate from Geisel's wartime mentality. But Dr. Seuss had to return to the psychic and material history embedded in *And to Think That I Saw It on Mulberry Street*, the scene of origin for all of Dr. Seuss's children's books, before he could release his art from the childhood memories that might otherwise continue to condition it. Dr. Seuss wrote a series of children's stories for *Redbook* that reported the "latest news from Mulberry street." "Marco Comes Late" recounts Marco's attempt to give a plausible reason for arriving more than two hours late for school.[47] Some of the Mulberry Street stories are concerned with more realistic themes. "How Officer Pat Saved the Whole Town" describes the stratagems a vigilant policeman devises to prevent "Mr. Schmitz" from detonating a dynamite truck in the center of town.[48] The continuing influence of these Mulberry Street memories on Dr. Seuss's art depends in part on the fact that Marco never in fact succeeds in going home, for his home lacks the capacity to make him feel as if he belongs there. It is only while he is in transit between home and school that Marco can liberate himself from the shame arising from his father's rebuke.

Dr. Seuss repeatedly restaged this origin story. He situated a different child in a different Springfield in each of three books—*McElligot's Pool* (1947), *If I Ran the Zoo* (1950), and *If I Ran the Circus* (1956)—that were set in the mythic Springfield of his youth. Each of the stories, which, along with *And to Think That I Saw It on Mulberry Street*, constitutes what might be called Dr. Seuss's Springfield cycle, enriches and is enriched by the others. Individually and in composite they are variations on Marco's compulsive need to enlarge upon his life until he works through the trauma of being unable to communicate with his father that started the compulsion. Dr. Seuss's completion of the cycle released him from the hold of the emotions that incited it.

In these works Dr. Seuss deploys a narrative structure that is different from the one at work in *Mulberry Street*, and he situates child protagonists in different relationships to their settings from that of Marco on Mulberry Street. *McElligot's Pool*, *If I Ran the Circus*, and *If I Ran the Zoo* are all concerned with places—the fishing hole, the zoo, the circus—that were sources of anxious pleasure when he was growing up. Although the pool, zoo, and circus resemble the Springfield locations on which they are modeled, they are unlike these historically factual places in that they give the child protagonists in the stories access to a realm of pure make-believe. The boys are different from Marco (and Ted) in that each one of them imagines himself celebrated as a hero by the townspeople and feels completely at home there.

Despite the difference in their time of composition, these works share a common structure. In each an adult poses either an explicit or implicit challenge to the child narrator, who responds with a series of increasingly fantastic scenarios. These later childhood stories achieve their spectacular effects by emulating the means whereby Marco suspended his father's prohibition. The

 phrase "If I Ran" in the titles of two of these books resembles Marco's "to think"; both introduce a hypothetical frame that suspends the provenance of the adult's insistence on empirically verifiable reality.

Dr. Seuss dedicated *McElligot's Pool* to Ted's father, "the world's greatest authority on

Blackfish, Fiddlercrabs and Deegel Trout."[49] The Deegel trout were trout that T. R. would purchase at the Deegel hatchery and pass off as trophies he and his son had actually caught. This was the only tall tale Geisel recalled his father telling.

The Marco of *McElligot's Pool* is unlike the Marco of *Mulberry Street* in that he manages to successfully explain his rationale for fishing. The farmer who observes the young boy attempting to fish issues a prediction that resembles the original father's admonition:

> If you sat fifty years
> With your worms and your wishes,
> You'd grow a long beard
> Long before you'd catch fishes!

Unlike his *Mulberry Street* namesake, however, Marco directly responds to the adult. He begins his answer with a gentle conces-sion to the improbability of catching a fish in a pool, but he quickly converts it into a more decisive statement of belief:

> There MIGHT be a pool,
>   like I've read of in
>   books,
> *Connected to one of those*
>   *underground brooks!* . . .
> One doesn't catch *this* kind
>   of fish as a rule,
> But the chances are fine in
>   McElligot's Pool!

His tale concludes with the farmer, who had earlier pronounced McElligot's venture a hopeless impossibility, looking on dumbfounded as Marco explains:

> And that's why I think
> That I'm not such a fool
> When I sit here and fish
> In McElligot's Pool.

In *If I Ran the Zoo* Gerald McGrew turns his fantasized takeover of the zoo into the means to win the approval of everyone he encounters. Rather then being afraid of the folks he meets on the street, Gerald transforms their potentially hostile looks into helpless wonder: the whole *world* will say, "Young McGrew's made his mark. / He's built a zoo better than Noah's whole Ark!"[50]

If I Ran the Circus, the last story in the Springfield cycle, brings

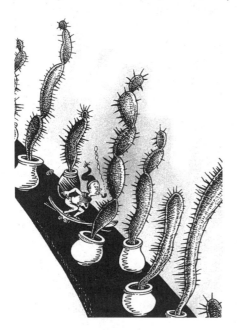

the saga full circle. It is the first of Dr. Seuss's books in which a child narrator includes an adult onlooker as a participant in his fantasy. Morris uses his imaginative powers to gratify his neighbor's unacknowledged need to achieve an elevation in self-worth. He accomplishes this by envisioning the "big vacant lot" behind Mr. Sneelock's modest store as the "most wonderful spot" for "The Circus McGurkus! The World's Greatest Show."

At first Mr. Sneelock's participation in Morris's adventure is modest. He helps out "doing small odds and ends." But Mr. Sneelock quickly turns into the star of the most dangerous and spectacular feats:

> This stunt is too grippingly, slippingly fright'ning!
> DOWN from the top of my tent like greased lightning
> Through pots full of lots of big Stickle-Bush Trees
> Slides a man! What a man! On his Roller-Skate-Skis![51]

The dedication to *If I Ran the Circus* reads, "This Book Is For My Dad Big Ted of Springfield The Finest Man I'll Evcr Know." By erecting a circus on its grounds, Morris redeems Mr. Sneelock's dilapidated vacant lot. Dr. Seuss's dedication of this book to "Big Ted of Springfield" metaphorically redeems the Geisel family's reputation. With the publication of this story, Dr. Seuss brought T. R. out of the backroom, where he had been

overheard "saying SOB, SOB over and over" and included him in the world of his art as the finest man his son would ever know.

The four Springfield cycle stories enabled Dr. Seuss to heal

Ted's emotional wounds by inventing spaces that lacked the hostile conditions that had motivated them. It is notable that *If I Ran the Zoo* and *If I Ran the Circus* contain images missing from *And to Think That I Saw It on Mulberry Street*: men identifiable as members of the German American community (the men wearing Homburg hats) and beer bottles of the same sort that would have been distributed by the Geisel family brewery.

THE TERWILLIKER DISASTER

Despite his reawakened interest in writing children's books, Geisel did not commit himself fully to this genre until 1953. In the early 1950s children's books competed with other outlets for his creative energies. In 1950 he promoted an idea to P. D. Eastman of United Production of America for an animated cartoon of a little boy who "didn't speak words but only weird sounds" that imitated such noises as horse neighs and car crashes.[52] Geisel wrote and produced what would become the Academy Award–winning *Gerald McBoing Boing*. Critics wrote that it raised the animator's ear to a higher plane.

He also wrote ads for Ford Motor Company, and in 1951 he accepted an advance of thirty-five thousand dollars to begin work on a feature-length fantasy film called *The 5,000 Fingers of Dr. T*. The film, which was released in 1953, opens with a little boy named Bartholomew, who is so bored with piano lessons that he falls asleep and dreams that he has traveled to a castle in which Dr. Terwilliker rules over a keyboard two stories high. Dr. Terwilliker has confined five hundred boys in his castle, and he threatens them with torture if they refuse to play his piano in their "lock-me-tights."

Dr. Terwilliker's grim demands for abject obedience recall Lord Droon in *The King's Stilts*. Dr. Terwilliker sees his piano racket as a scheme for global domination in the Terwilliker Empire for Tomorrow. The actor Hans Conried played Dr. Terwilliker; the freedom-loving, all-American boy, Bart, was played by Tommy Rettig from the popular television series *Lassie*.

In the film's climactic moment Bart awakens his widowed mother from Terwilliker's spell and leads the boys in a successful rebellion against the villain with the following lyrics:

Because we're closer to the ground.
And you are bigger pound by pound.
You have no right, you have no right
To push and shove us little kids around.[53]

Geisel wrote the lyrics, screenplay, and sketchbooks for the film, which he desperately wanted to be a success. But the producers' repeated demands for revisions led to his loss of control over the production. The final cut was worse than he feared. He described the making of *The 5,000 Fingers of Dr. T* as the "down period" of his career: "As to who was most responsible for this debaculous fiasco, I will have nothing more to say until all the participants have passed away, including myself."[54]

The movie failed at the box office, and when his agent, Phyllis Jackson, brought him an idea for an educational television series in 1953, he rejected it: "It's been seven years since I gave up being a soldier. . . . Now I'd like to give up movies and advertising and anything else that means dueling with vice-presidents and committees, hmmm?. . . I want to stay in La Jolla and write children's books. . . . If I dropped everything else do you think I could count on royalties of 5000 dollars a year?"[55] Jackson responded that given his reputation and the baby boom, five thousand dollars a year seemed reasonable.

Dr. Seuss's Reunion

In the early 1950s Geisel felt that he needed to make amends for the anti-Japanese vitriol in his *PM* cartoons and in the film *Know Your Enemy—Japan*, which was released to the troops on August 16, 1945, the day the United States dropped the bomb on Nagasaki. Japan surrendered six days after the film was released. Geisel began to revise the film after he accepted an invitation from RKO to do an adaptation of it. Helen assisted with the film script, which highlighted the theme of seven centuries of authoritarian rule. The documentary was released in 1947 as *Design for Death*, with Hans Conried playing the voice of Japan. The film won the Oscar for best documentary. *Design for Death* closed with a call for a more democratic postwar culture and focused on "the problem of educating our kids—*all* our kids—to be smarter than we've been."[56]

The Geisels accepted an offer from *Life* magazine to go to Japan to research the American occupation's impact on educational and child-rearing practices and to learn how those practices changed the ambitions of Japan's children. They sailed on March 24, 1953. Their trip permitted Geisel to atone for the racist and xenophobic sentiments in his World War II cartoons. After World War II Japan and Korea had adopted *And to Think That I Saw It on Mulberry Street* and *The 500 Hats of Bartholomew Cubbins* as part of their postwar elementary curriculum. Geisel's former classmate, Donald Bartlett, asked friends with diplomatic ties to arrange for teachers in Kyoto, Osaka, and Kobe to assist the Geisels with their research by asking their students to draw pictures of what they hoped to be when they grew up. Most boys wanted to be aviators or to go to Mars; most girls wanted to be hostesses on interurban buses.[57] The Geisels published the results of their research in *Life* magazine as "Japan's Young Dreams." But the publisher, Henry Luce, who "was always anti-Japanese and pro-Chinese," called for extensive revisions of every aspect of the Geisels' essay. Not only did the *Life* staff substitute "conclusions of their own not warranted by the facts," but they also featured photographs that distorted the realities of postwar Japanese culture. "Very few children drew themselves in Oriental clothing but those few formed a high proportion of those published by *Life*," Geisel complained.[58]

In the fall of 1953 Geisel began another book on Horton the elephant. This one drew on his recently acquired knowledge of Japan's schools, where individualism was a relatively new concept. He dedicated *Horton Hears a Who* to a Kyoto educator named Mitsugi Nakamura whom he had met during his trip. According to the Seuss scholar Henry Jenkins, Geisel intended *Horton Hears a Who* to be used to train "children in emerging democratic cultures around the world, about the relationship between the individual and the community."[59]

Having abandoned Horton to go to war, Geisel expressed his complete fidelity to the work of writing of children's books by returning to him. Horton is representative of the animals in Dr. Seuss's children's books, who differ from those in his satiric cartoons in that they do not allegorize Geisel's ideological attitudes. Dr. Seuss's animal stories should be interpreted according to the quality the eponymous animal personifies. Each animal personifies a trait—Horton the elephant's concern, Thidwick the moose's hospitality, Yertle the turtle's arrogance—whose cultural consequences the story explores. In giving these deeply felt affects an animated form, Dr. Seuss turns interiorized human emotions into objects for conscious deliberation. Each animal's story encapsulates a mood that produces an emotional effect on the audience. "None of my animals are animals," Geisel said. "They're all people sort of."[60]

In *Horton Hatches the Egg* Horton risked lifelong captivity rather than go back on his word. The Horton who hears a Who becomes involved in a comparable ordeal. After Horton discerns the nearly inaudible voices of people who live on a microscopic speck on top of a dandelion, he risks everything in his effort to persuade the other members of his culture that these persons exist. Interpretations of *Horton Hears a Who* normally begin with the assumption that Dr. Seuss's sole intention in writing it was to encourage tolerance for the Japanese. Horton's maxim "A person's a person no matter how small" is taken to be a rhymed plea for minority rights. But the story is somewhat more complicated than these explanations suggest.

According to Jenkins, when Horton listens to the all but imperceptible yelp of the Whos' civilization, he is "caught between two different democratic communities." Jenkins believes that these community lines are clearly drawn: "On the one hand there is the conformist world of his [Horton's] own friends and neighbors.... On the other hand, there is the civic-minded community of Whoville.... Faced by a crisis that threatens their survival, the Whos rally together to insure that their voices are heard."[61]

There is no question that Horton experiences anguish after being cast out by his jungle community. But Dr. Seuss does not draw the lines of demarcation between these communities as starkly as Jenkins has. When the Kangaroo upbraids Horton, she does so in part because she believes that he has violated one of the principles that has kept the jungle peaceful. "Such carryings-on in our peaceable jungle! / We've had quite enough of your bellowing bungle!"[62]

The Kangaroo's hostile reaction to what she considers a fantasy resembles the antipathy to make-believe expressed by numerous other Dr. Seuss characters. But Horton has not in fact imagined hearing the Whos, and he needs the support of the rest of the jungle community to ensure Whoville's survival. Rather

than soliciting a belief in fantasy, as Marco does, Horton wants the other members of his jungle community to acknowledge the factual existence of the Whos.

Unable to hear the Whos, the Kangaroo considers Horton's claim to be a threat to the jungle peace. Although Horton cannot demonstrate the existence of the Whos to the other members of his community, he nevertheless asks the community to assist him in their protection. Were the community to collaborate in the protection of persons they can neither see nor hear, they would be participating in the construction of what the Kangaroo considers a collective delusion. In doing that, they would also violate the principle of reciprocal understanding crucial to keeping the jungle "peaceable."

When Jenkins contrasted the Kangaroo and the Whos, he described the latter as a "civic-minded" community whose members face this crisis by rallying together to make certain that "their voices are heard."

> "This," cried the mayor, "is your town's darkest hour!
> The time for all *Whos* who have blood that is red
> To come to the aid of their country!" he said.

The Whos have indeed rallied to confront this crisis, which Horton's protectionism is in part responsible for causing. But the readers have no way of knowing whether the Whos' communal concern preceded this event. When the mayor of Whoville drags Jo-Jo, the smallest Who of them all, out of his apartment and demands that he add his voice to the collective outcry, he has compelled the "smallest of the small" members of Whoville to join in the aid of a country that took no notice of his existence before this moment.

According to Jenkins, Horton expresses a nostalgia for the "Whoville-like America of the war years, when political differences were forgotten in the name of a common cause and fear over the rigid Wickersham-like conformity of the 1950s."[63] But Horton's community cannot know whether what he says he hears is real until they can hear what he hears. The fact that Horton struggles to make what he hears answerable to standards of evidence indicates that he has acknowledged the importance of communicating with his jungle peers.

Horton Hears a Who is organized as a rite of initiation. Being an outcast, Horton becomes a crucial bearer of the principle of concern vital to both the individual's and the community's development. By bringing what he knows into a form of knowledge that everyone in the community can share, he transforms the entire community. The knowledge that he now shares with the Kangaroo and the Wickershams is that communal care is a principle that applies to the smallest (least socialized and most minoritized) individual's relationship to the community as well as to the larger community's attitude toward the least recognized (hence most minoritized) of its members.

Jo-Jo is the representative within the Whoville community of a minoritized individual who has not received the community's acknowledgment. The Who responsible for the redemptive audibility of the entire Who community is also the one with the least audible voice within their society. Were it not for the grave danger to Whoville's survival posed by the Kangaroo's demand for proof of Whoville's existence, Jo-Jo might never have even been asked to participate in the community's song.

Jo-Jo's position within Whoville is comparable to Horton's within his jungle culture. Like Horton, Jo-Jo had to be heard before he could join the community of voices. In a sense Jo-Jo and Horton are versions of one another. Both represent excluded members who, when added to the community, change the whole social order.

After the Kangaroo judge and her Wickersham police finally are able to hear the Whos, they also hear (in the sense that they make it a social reality) communal care as the deepest principle of their community. Their need to hear and to be heard is gratified by Jo-Jo, whose "yopp" brings about a spontaneous shift in their perspective from intolerance toward an alien world to mutual care as a universal principle of community.

Most interpretations of *Horton Hears a Who* assign Horton an ideological stance that is opposed to the Kangaroo's. But the children's books Dr. Seuss published throughout the cold war—from *The Sneetches* to *The Butter Battle Book*—subverted the need to organize social life in terms of such intractable ideological oppositions. *Horton Hears a Who* renews both

communities because every person in each community now affirms a moral principle that everyone can hear and understand. Whoville and Hortonville share the condition of having moved from communities organized around the principle of "All but one" to the compound principle "One for all and all for one another." Horton has simplified this compound principle into the maxim "A person's a person no matter how small."[64]

Four

DR. SEUSS AND HELEN GEISEL'S EMPIRE

THE CAT'S HOUSE

The circumstances surrounding the publication of *The Cat in the Hat* are well known. William Spaulding, who met Geisel during his stay at Fort Fox, had become the director of Houghton Mifflin's educational division of children's books. Spaulding challenged Geisel to write a primer of no more than 225 unique words to be selected from a list of 348. He also wanted a book that first-graders would be unable to put down. Bennett Cerf agreed to permit Geisel to write the reader for Houghton Mifflin, under the condition that they publish only the school edition; Random House retained the right to market the trade editions in bookstores. After its publication, however, Spaulding wrangled with Cerf over trade rights to the book. Cerf won the battle after Houghton Mifflin encountered some unexpected trouble selling the book to schools. "There were lots of Dick and Jane devotees," Geisel explained, "and my book was considered too fresh and irreverent."[1] But Cerf's trade edition took off in bookstores. On March 1, 1957, Random House published twelve thousand copies of the book, priced at two dollars. Unlike their teachers, the six- and seven-year-olds who heard about the book from their friends nagged until their parents bought them a copy. According to Geisel's biographers, *The Cat in the Hat* was the first book to become a "playground word-of-mouth" best-seller.[2] The first printing sold so well that Random House ordered a second in April. The book's average sales were twelve thousand copies a month. Within three years Random House had sold nearly a million copies, and editions were available in French, Chinese, Swedish, and Braille. Ellen Lewis Buell's March 17 notice in the *New York Times Book Review* was representative of the critical reaction. She described *The Cat in the Hat* as "one of the most original and funniest of books for early readers." She added, "Beginning readers and parents who have been helping them through the dreary activities of Dick and Jane and other primer characters are due for a happy surprise." The *New Yorker*'s Ellen Maxwell described it as the "sort of book children insist on taking to bed with them." In an article entitled "The Significance of Dr. Seuss" that he published in *The New York Times Book Review*, David Dempsey declared it the "biggest thing that happened to the American classroom since the McGuffey's reader in 1836."[3]

The origins of *The Cat in the Hat* hark back to an article entitled "Why Do Children Bog Down in the First R?" (a reference to reading, writing, and arithmetic) that John Hersey published in the May 1954 issue of *Life*. Hersey characterized "bland idealized primers like Dick and Jane" as the bearers of the primary responsibility for illiteracy in America. He singled out Dr. Seuss as one of "the wonderfully imaginative geniuses among children's illustrators" who were imagining something new to replace them. Hersey pointed out that such children's books had to go up against "television, radio, movies, comic books, magazines, and sports. . . . This is hard competition because most commonplace pictures demand only the act of looking, while words, to mean anything, demand an act of imagination."[4]

Dr. Seuss accepted Spaulding's challenge because he shared Hersey's concern. Overthrowing the stupefying banality of *Dick and Jane* readers, *The Cat in the Hat* was a book that could finally compete with the comics and animated cartoons. But the book's success was not accidental. Before writing it, Dr. Seuss analyzed the reading process, particularly the part that pertained to a child's ability to correlate words with the images and sounds that made them legible.[5] Why should Johnny want to read when he could be watching television, or playing with his friends, or tearing around the house? Rather than avoid these questions, Dr. Seuss incorporated them into the plot of *The Cat in the Hat*. The book opens with two children, Sally and an unnamed boy we'll call Johnny, sitting mesmerized in front of a window whose panes resemble blank television screens.

The Cat in the Hat alters the Dr. Seuss formula, which begins with a child's feeling of discontent with his mundane circumstances. The discontent typically motivates the child protagonist to visualize an alternative world. What Marco saw on Mulberry Street, what Gerald McGrew encountered at the zoo, what Morris McGurk envisioned behind Mr. Sneelock's store, and what Marco's counterpart glimpsed within McElligot's pool supplanted their impoverished reality. These child protagonists turned ordinary activities into occasions to see what they *might* have seen.

At the conclusions of these stories the children reaffirm the difference between the worlds they have and the ones they have imagined by returning to the world as it appeared at the outset. These visual excursions do not undermine the children's relationship to reality.[6] They confirm the order of things by adding the pleasure of make-believe. These children know that the world to which they have returned can be reanimated whenever they choose to exercise their imagination. After they add these *as if* dimensions to what the world *as is* lacks, these children return to a real world that their imaginative activities have enhanced.[7]

The Cat in *The Cat in the Hat* bears a resemblance to other figures in Dr. Seuss's menagerie: the giraffe from *And to Think That I Saw It on Mulberry Street*, the Thingamajigger from *McElligot's Pool*, the Bippo no Bungus from *If I Ran the Zoo*, the Whos Horton hears. Moreover Sally and Johnny resemble other human children in Dr. Seuss's tales who feel trapped in a world lacking the enlivening powers of the imagination. But Dr. Seuss added variations to *The Cat in the Hat* that significantly altered his formula.

The Cat in the Hat is the first book in which the imagined figures that the child protagonists perceive are not the inventions of the children. Dr. Seuss's previous narrators sustained their imagined world on the condition that they remained unnoticed by the creatures within it. But the Cat actively involves Sally and Johnny in his games and entertains them with the things he brings with him. By the same token Johnny and Sally, unlike Marco, actively participate in the Cat's make-believe world.

Johnny and Sally also differ from Dr. Seuss's previous child protagonists in that they undergo a decisive change in their relationship to the Cat's imagined world, and unlike the other narrators they undergo this change from within the safe environs of their home. Whereas in the beginning the children are ambivalent about the Cat's prospective games, they conclude by ordering him to pick up his things and get out of their house:

> Then I said to the cat,
> "Now you do as I say.
> You take up those things
> And you take them away!"[8]

Despite these crucial distinctions, *The Cat in the Hat* also resembles its precursors: it begins with a circumstance that clearly demarcates the children's everyday world from the alternative reality of the Cat. The book opens with a factual state of affairs: Johnny and Sally's mother has gone out. It is raining, and so it is too wet and cold to go outside to play. They watch the rain, which prevents their using the outdoor playthings—a bicycle, a kite, and balls and gloves—lined up neatly against the wall. So Sally and Johnny are compelled to sit in the house and wish they "had something to do!" The distinction between the world they have and what they wish for emerges when suddenly "something went BUMP!"

Abruptly the Cat comes in from the rain, seemingly from right out of an animated cartoon. Standing upright, he is carrying an umbrella along with magical playthings and games that do not leave a mess for Sally and Johnny to clean up.

We looked!
Then we saw him step in on the mat!
We looked!
And we saw him!
The Cat in the Hat!

The "BUMP!" is all the more remarkable because it lacks a determinate cause and arouses the children's need to find one. Their need for an explanation releases their power of visual imagination—"We looked!"—that renders them receptive to numerous possible explanations that might make sense of the noise. The Cat has entered the children's time and the household's space through a breach that has momentarily opened because of the incomprehensible sound.

The narrative proper begins when a fish in a bowl responds to the children's complaint that there's nothing for us to do on this "cold, cold, wet day" with the admonition "He should not be here. / He should not be about. / He should not be here / When your mother is out!"[9] Under constant threat of being thrown out of the water by the Cat, the fish has the most to lose from his presence.

In his first game, the Cat does what the fish says he mustn't:

"Up-Up-Up with a fish!"

"Put me down!" said the fish.
"This is no fun at all!"

In this passage the Cat addresses the fear his uninvited entrance may have aroused in Johnny and Sally. Children are not supposed to let strangers into their house. The Cat has not only come in un-invited; he has brought a box with him containing the somewhat sinister Thing One and Thing Two.[10] After gaining entrance the Cat creates a drama that distracts the children from their

anxiety. He makes himself a constant source of fun rather then a figure to fear. Only the fish expresses fright. The fish, a surrogate for the absent mother, invokes her authority to admonish the children against violating household rules.

The children's pleasure comes in part from the Cat's disobeying the fish's instructions. Their pleasure specifically derives from the juxtaposition of possible causes of this loud noise to the spectacularly improbable explanations that the Cat acts out. The loud bump could have been caused by a domestic cat's having knocked over the fishbowl, or toppled pots from a table, or pushed toys off a chest, or brushed books from a shelf.[11] The Cat immediately transposes all of these possible explanations into the juggling act, which constitutes the first of his performances.

From the outset the Cat seems in the grip of a delirium of self-theatricalizing enjoyment that he wants to communicate to Sally and Johnny. But what does the Cat want from them? From the moment he enters the house the Cat communicates the desire to connect the words that he speaks with the things that he does. In motivating the children to make this connection, this strange animal demands that the children look at him as he expresses himself through speech acts that do what he says.

Apprehending the Cat requires that the children recognize how he is different from domestic cats. He is composed of words, images, rhyming word-images, and the reflexive process that interconnects them. His name attaches a word (Cat) to another pictured word (Hat) that rhymes. But making this connection requires a set of distinctions between two word-images (the Cat, the Hat) that rhyme yet are slightly different. The concatenation of the phrase "in the Hat" and "Cat" requires an imaginative double-take to correlate an already existing perceptual image, a cat, to an anomaly, a creature standing upright at the doorway wearing a bowtie and stovepipe hat. Although the children have not imagined him, the Cat nevertheless requires their continued imaginative activity to remain within their environment. In order to see the Cat the children must suspend disbelief. Under constant threat of erasure, the Cat depends on the collusion of the children's imagination to remain in their world.

The scenarios he acts out gratify the children's wish for something to do while their mother is out. Rather than erasing him, Sally and Johnny at first participate in the remarkable scenarios that the Cat opens up within their house. He puts these games into play by way of sentences that do the things he says as he is doing them. These games and the sentences through which he plays them would never have appeared in a *Dick and Jane* reader.

In the following passage the Cat is at once an image, a series of activities, a way of speaking that does what he says, and a way of correlating the words that he says with the illustrations of him doing what he says.

> "Look at me!
> Look at me now!" said the cat.
> "With a cup and a cake
> On the top of my hat!
> I can hold up TWO books!
> I can hold up the fish!
> And a little toy ship!
> And some milk on a dish!"

Reading differs from simply looking at an image because it includes the reflexive knowledge of what is perceived. The Cat's initial demand "Look at me now!" urgently draws the children to an immediate perception. As the Cat subsequently repeats the

phrase "Look at me!" he oversees the transition from seeing to reading by implanting the desire to learn how to participate in the process whereby he does what he is saying. He acts as an image that performs the reflexive relation to the words through which he becomes imaginable. What takes place in this transition between looking and reading is the Cat's performance of the relation between images and words.

Each time this sensuous image shouts "Look at me!" he seems to take pleasure in being read. Repeating the phrase opens up space and makes time for the reader to connect the pictures of things with the printed words; thus the pictured things become at once audible and legible. His onlookers can only fulfill the demand "Look at me! / Look at me! / Look at me NOW!" by learning how to connect the images of the things that the Cat is juggling with the words that he shouts out as he juggles them. With each "Look at me!" he communicates the desire to learn how to read. Indeed the Cat might be described as the activity of reading personified.

The interval from one series of activities that begins with "Look at me!" to the next resonates with the echoes of words that are repeated in rhyming anapests. Every word in the series contains the trace of a perceivable image through which it becomes imaginable, and every image contains the trace of the word through which it becomes audible. Reading is the creative force that allows for the exchange of these traces between image and word. Each unknown word sounds like the rhyme word that precedes it and conforms to the accentual pattern of the line. Children learn the sound of a new word by way of a rhyming word. The end rhymes of *cat* and *hat*, *cake* and *rake*, *man* and *fan*, *fish* and *dish*, *ball* and *all*, and the internal rhymes *cup* and *up* and *looks* and *books* assist the reader in pronouncing the unknown words.[12]

Geisel said he added this juggling scene to bring in a series of required nouns, "cup, milk, cake, rake, toy, fan," that he could not have otherwise included. But as he takes up these words and juggles them off the page, the Cat teaches children how language works. Learning how to read these words involves hearing how the words sound. The rhymes and rhythms of which the passage is composed facilitate this instruction.

After the Cat includes the children in the spectacles he enacts, they find themselves within the scene of reading in which they are at once participants and observers. The Cat cannot write, and the children cannot read. He needs the children to learn how to perform the connection between the images that he is juggling with the words and pictures through which they become intelligible so that he can remain a legible presence within their world.

The Cat in the Hat is the classic in the archive of Dr. Seuss stories for which it serves as a cornerstone and a linchpin. Before writing it Geisel was better known for the ad campaign "Quick, Henry, the Flit" than for his nine children's books. The unimaginable success of the book replaced Geisel with the iconic figure Dr. Seuss as the persona responsible for its creation. In doing what *Dick and Jane* readers failed to do—make Johnny want to learn how to read—*The Cat in the Hat* propelled Dr. Seuss into the center of the most important academic controversy of the cold war.

Prior to the book's 1957 publication, Geisel was making slightly more from the royalties on his other books than the five thousand dollars a year he had designated as his desired annual income. *The Cat in the Hat* dramatically increased the sales of all of his previous publications. In 1940, the year after its initial publication, Random House sold 394 copies of *The King's Stilts*. But in 1958 sales jumped to 11,037, and by 1960 they had climbed to nearly 75,000. Sales of the other books followed a similar trajectory. Customers purchased 5,801 copies of *Horton Hatches the Egg* in 1940; the following year sales fell to 1,645. But in 1958 Random House sold 27,643 copies of *Horton Hatches the Egg*, and in 1960 its total sales leaped to a whopping 200,000. *The Cat in the Hat* made the Geisels a fortune.

Dr. Seuss's Other Hand

From the time of their wedding, Helen had been a partner in Ted's creative activities. She critiqued the coherence of his narratives, questioned the aptness of his illustrations, proposed alternative scenes, invented new characters, revised his sentences, and let him know when a story sounded finished enough to be named one of their imaginary children. She was even more important to the running of Ted's practical world. He did not know how to make coffee, cook, or manage a checkbook. From the day in 1926 when she saw him draw winged cows in place of lecture notes at Oxford, Helen decided to shield Ted from the responsibilities of the real world. All of this came to an abrupt end in 1954.

Shortly after distribution of the *The 5000 Fingers of Dr. T* in May of that year Helen began to experience a frightening form of physical debilitation. It started with numbness in her ankles, then spread throughout her body. When Geisel took her to the San Diego County Hospital the doctors placed her in an iron lung. After performing a tracheotomy to facilitate her breathing, they told Geisel that the likelihood of her surviving what they diagnosed as Guillain-Barré syndrome was uncertain.[13] For the next five months, as Geisel sat vigil at her hospital bedside, Helen did not seem to recognize him.

In the hope of lifting her spirits he constructed a relay of mirrors from her iron lung to the hospital window so that she could see the image of their dog Cluny. Toward the end of June doctors told him that her condition had improved enough for them to remove the tracheotomy tube. On July 4 medical staff transported Helen to a swimming pool for therapeutic water exercise. Within the year she had made a spectacular recovery.

In May 1955 the couple flew to New Hampshire to celebrate the thirtieth reunion of the Dartmouth class of 1925 and for Geisel to receive an honorary doctorate in the company of Robert Frost. Rather than attach the new honorific to his given name, Geisel remarked that he might now be required to sign his works Dr. Dr. Seuss. The citation for his doctorate of letters reads in part, "As author and artist you single-handedly have stood as St. George between a generation of exhausted parents and the demon-dragon of unexhausted children on a rainy day."[14]

President John Sloan Dickey's citation was worded to acknowledge Geisel's artistic accomplishments. But neither "demon-dragon" nor "single-handedly" accurately described Ted Geisel's work. He had coproduced almost all of his books with Helen. Moreover it would take him another year and a half to invent the Cat that the phrase "demon-dragon of unexhausted children on a rainy day" prefigured.

Nevertheless the term "single-handedly" did attest to the strategy Geisel had devised to ward off fears provoked by Helen's illness. In most of the published discussions of his mode of artistic production prior to 1955 Geisel acknowledged the key role that Helen played as a collaborator in his creative process. "She's a hard task master," he remarked in a 1953 interview. "Here I sit up all night writing that stuff, and she tears it to pieces the next morning. But she's a great editor and condenser. I couldn't get along without her."[15]

Dedicating *The 500 Hats of Bartholomew Cubbins* to their imaginary child "Chrysanthemum-Pearl" may have sounded like a good joke, but in a note that she addressed to classmates in the *Wellesley Record Book of 1953* Helen represented the results of their artistic collaborations as substitutes for the children she was physically unable to conceive: "All of you who have children and even grandchildren to report on have a wide scope of activities. We have never caught up with you biologically, and thus our annals are scant. Our life is still very much centered around Ted's drawing board, and the metamorphoses of blank sheets of paper into sensible nonsense."[16]

After Helen's recovery, however, Geisel increasingly preferred to work alone. Robert Bernstein, who would succeed Bennett Cerf at Random House, later reported, "The more I saw of him, the more he liked being in that room and creating all by himself."[17] In Bernstein's opinion "single-handedly" also became an appropriate description of their marriage.

Throughout the eighteen months that it took to complete, Geisel preferred to work alone on *The Cat in the Hat*. After its publication he and Cerf declared it the inaugural volume in a new series for children just learning to read. The Beginner Books series was intended to attract writers who shared Dr. Seuss's pedagogical interests. Although he would regularly contribute new books to the series, Geisel asked Helen to assume primary responsibility for the acquisition, editing, and rejection of the manuscripts submitted for publication. Over the next ten years she actively solicited new manuscripts for Beginner Books, wrote letters asking for revision, published her own books in the series, and kept track of the income that it earned for the Ted and Helen Geisel charities.[18]

Random House published *How the Grinch Stole Christmas!* in 1957, shortly after publishing *The Cat in the Hat*. Geisel used the book, which attracted a comparably large readership, to distinguish between Beginner Books and what he now chose to call his Big Books.[19] *The Cat in the Hat* taught children the fun of learning how to read by offering a subject about which they wanted to read. Big Books differed only in that they supplied subject matter with more content. The idea was that once children learned how to "play" with language they could move on to books that were closer to literature in scope. In writing these Big Books Dr. Seuss fulfilled a wish he had initially formulated as a undergraduate. He was now writing Great Literature with a capital G and a capital L.

DR. SEUSS'S BIG BOOKS

The protagonist of *How the Grinch Stole Christmas!* inhabits the more expansive imaginary terrain populated by literary archetypes. Like Ebenezer Scrooge and Old St. Nick, the Grinch has become inextricably affiliated with the holiday he tried to steal. What happens to him after he fails fills in the heart of the book.

Living all alone just North of Whoville, the Grinch thinks that the Whos' materialism constitutes the sole meaning of their Christmas celebrations. His resentment arises from his exclusion from the festivities. In retaliation he sneaks into Whoville and carries away all the food, presents, and decorations with which the Whos celebrate Christmas. Of course, as we all know well by now, even after the Grinch steals all of the Whos' Christmas stuff, Christmas comes anyway. His effort to steal Christmas thereby uncovers a Christmas that can neither be given nor taken: " 'Maybe Christmas,' he thought, *'doesn't* come from a store. / Maybe Christmas ... perhaps ... means a little bit more!' "[20]

The Grinch steals Christmas because he wants to enjoy the pain the Whos will suffer at the loss of their gifts, food, and furnishings. But the Whos are, in fact, ultimately indifferent to the commercialized version seized by the Grinch. Indeed it is only after the Grinch successfully carries away all the material goods

of Christmas that the Whos come together as a true community. In becoming the grounds of the festivities rather than a figure who is included or excluded from them, the Grinch binds the Who community to the deep fellowship that the exchange of gifts signifies.

When the Grinch witnesses the real basis of an otherwise

commercialized cultural economy, he undergoes a transformation. The irony of *How the Grinch Stole Christmas!* is that by taking all the things, the Grinch becomes the measure of the generosity that Christmas upholds. As the connection between the beneficence of Christmas and the commercial enterprise through which it circulates, the Grinch no longer feels excluded from the society but is re-created by it. His new way of perceiving the Whos changes the way that the Grinch and the Whos determine gains and losses.

In writing a book that explores the cultural significance of this religious holiday Dr. Seuss addressed one of Great Literature's largest questions—What are the ties that bind human beings? Over the next ten years he published six more Big Books: *Yertle the Turtle and Other Stories* (1958), *Happy Birthday to You* (1959), *The Sneetches and Other Stories* (1961), *Dr. Seuss's Sleep Book* (1962), *I Had Trouble in Getting to Solla Sollew* (1965), and *The Cat in the Hat Songbook* (1967). At least two of them tackled comparably monumental subjects.

In *Yertle the Turtle and Other Stories* Dr. Seuss addressed a subject that would preoccupy him throughout the cold war: social and political hierarchy. King Yertle is not content to exercise rule over the pond in which he resides on the island of Sala-ma-Sond. He wants to become the ruler over all that he sees. This desire can be gratified only by commanding the other turtles in the pond to stand on one another's backs so as to extend the reach of King Yertle's empire vertically until he can declare, "There's nothing, no, NOTHING, that's higher than me!"[21]

However, because Yertle's empire is literally stacked upon the backs of the turtles under his dominion, his rule cannot outlast his subjects' willingness to withstand the oppressive weight. A plain little turtle named Mack articulates the turtles' natural rights: "I know up on top you are seeing great sights / but down at the bottom we, too, should have rights." After King Yertle refuses to recognize the other turtles' right to live without the pain and the hunger brought on by his oppressive order, Mack's body gives biopolitical expression to his distress: "*He burped!*" This very natural disturbance brings the precarious stack of turtles tumbling down.

The dependence of King Yertle's power on the least empowered of his subjects reiterates two invariant themes of Dr. Seuss's beast books: the reversibility of power and the need for communal interdependence. King Yertle's lack of concern for his subjects' welfare reveals what's wrong with his governance. In articulating the dis-ease inhabiting the body politic, Mack's burp enacts the right to physical welfare that pertains to every person, no matter how lowly. Furthermore it transforms King Yertle's pond into a society in which all turtles are free.

> And today the great Yertle, that Marvelous he,
> Is King of the Mud. That is all he can see.
> And the turtles, of course . . . all the turtles are free
> As turtles and, maybe, all creatures should be.

Though *Yertle the Turtle and Other Stories* was published in 1958, the book was widely reviewed as a postwar critique of Hitler's authoritarian rule. And when *The Sneetches and Other Stories* appeared three years later critics saw its antiracist theme as an elaboration of the critique of anti-Semitism that Geisel had directed against Nazi Germany in his work at *PM*.[22] The Sneetches belong to a society whose exclusionary practices are based on physical differences: some Sneetches are born with

little stars on their bellies, others are not. The Sneetches with stars maintain their social domination through oppressive processes of subordination and exclusion. The Nazis use of yellow stars to stigmatize Jews supplied these interpretations with seemingly indisputable evidence. But the reading of this book as an unproblematic critique of anti-Semitism did not go unchallenged. Indeed Bernstein famously recalled Geisel telling him why he was going to abandon the book: "Someone I respect told me it was anti-Semitic." To which Bernstein responded, "How can a man of your tremendous accomplishments be so jarred by one stupid comment?"[23] Bernstein's rejoinder persuaded Geisel that the criticism lacked substance. But the intensity of Geisel's reaction and his readiness to abandon the project reveals his continued need to completely renounce his earlier anti-Semitic work.

The Sneetches are personifications of social affects in which envy, exclusivity, and aggression are intertwined. Rather than adopting a position that was for or against the Sneetches with or without little stars, Dr. Seuss disparaged the need to embrace either of these positions. The Sneetches remain trapped in a destructive social structure until they arrive at a shared recognition: their need for a social order grounded in exclusionary oppositions victimizes both the Sneetches with and the Sneetches without stars.

> The day they decided that Sneetches are Sneetches
> And no kind of Sneetch is the best on the beaches.
> That day, all the Sneetches forgot about stars
> And whether they had one or not, upon thars.[24]

Green Eggs and Ham

By engaging the themes of social discrimination and minority rights in the Big Books that he published after *How the Grinch*

Stole Christmas! Dr. Seuss made good on his commitment to write socially transformative children's books. *Yertle the Turtle* and *The Sneetches* demonstrated how Dr. Seuss's imagined worlds could emancipate adults from the intractable oppositions underpinning their social order. While he supplied his Big Books with subject matter that was consonant with his belief that "books for Children have a greater potential for good, or evil, than any other form of literature on earth," the Beginner Books division of his enterprise did not receive a comparable visionary investment until Random House published *Green Eggs and Ham* in 1960.

The Cat in the Hat inaugurated Beginner Books with an iconic masterwork in 1957, but its subject seemed idiosyncratic rather than exemplary. When Dr. Seuss published *The Cat in the Hat Comes Back* in 1958 the sequel seemed a disappointing repetition of its precursor's structure rather than a renewal of vision. The Beginner Book that succeeded in revitalizing the series was in part the result of a challenge that was even more daunting than the one William Spaulding had posed to Geisel five years earlier.

Dr. Seuss began work on *Green Eggs and Ham* after Bennett Cerf bet him fifty dollars that he could not write a book with fewer than fifty words that would make six-year-olds want to learn to read all by themselves. This vocabulary limitation much exceeded *The Cat in the Hat* in severity. In his efforts to win, Dr. Seuss turned the extreme limitations his publisher had placed on the book's form into the inspiration to discover and exploit hidden linguistic resources.

Organized as a cumulative dramatic sequence that unfolds around a simple question-and-answer format, *Green Eggs and*

Ham places fifty-one different words in patterned combinations within verse stanzas composed of rhyming anapests. All of the book's 681 words are easy to understand; its sentences are brief; its action is funny; its rhythm is catchy; and its pictures are eye-grabbing.

The story tracks the efforts undertaken by a young Grinch-like creature named Sam-I-Am to persuade an un-named adult to try the green eggs and ham that he offers on a platter. The scenario mirrors one that is quite familiar to children who find repulsive the greens—spinach, broccoli, or peas—that adults unfailingly place before them. But usually the demand comes from the adult and is directed at the child.

When Sam-I-Am attempts to persuade the adult to try the seemingly noxious dish, he is answered by a series of rejections. But he refuses to take no for an answer. In this exchange it is the adult who must accede to the demands of the child. Rather than offering some rationale for this change in the positions of power, the younger Sam-I-Am instead repeatedly relocates the adult in a space in which he tests the conditions of the rejection: "Would you eat it in . . . ?" or "Would you eat it with . . . ?" Sam-I-Am's many ripostes reverse the role played by the child narrator in *And to Think That I Saw It on Mulberry Street*, for his increasingly outlandish scenarios finally compel his adult antagonist to retract his rejection.

Except for the negation at work in the adult's statements, the characters' declarations create an echo. The adult is adamant in his rejection. But Sam-I-Am, obstinate and persevering, finally wears him down. The adult's answers re-cite elements of Sam-I-Am's questions until finally the adult's "I do not like" becomes

"I like" because he has exhausted the possible places in which he can give reasonable expression to disliking green eggs and ham:

> Adult: I would not like them
> here or there.
> I would not like them
> anywhere.
>
> Sam-I-am: You do not like them.
> So you say.
> Try them! Try them!
> And you may.
> Try them and you may, I say.[25]

Sam-I-Am's counterpart can no longer say no to green eggs and ham after he topples from the boat in which he has refused the penultimate offer of the dish.

Upon reaching shore Sam-I-Am's companion concedes, "If you let me be, I will try them." He thereby produces the common ground that was missing from their initial encounter. Once he has located this common ground, the adult's decision to eat the dish results in the discovery that he does indeed like green eggs and ham.

> Adult: I do so like
> Green eggs and ham!
> Thank you!
> Thank you,
> Sam-I-Am!

Geisel may have written *Green Eggs and Ham* as a tour de force designed to win a bet, but like *The Cat in the Hat* it exceeded the terms of the challenge. The book successfully closes the gap separating the limited interests of six-year-olds from the reading matter that addresses those interests. *Green Eggs and Ham* meets those interests by transporting one of the themes Dr. Seuss explored in his Big Books—the deep social bond concealed beneath socially entrenched antagonisms—into what would quickly became the most popular of his Beginner Books.

Most of the books published under the Beginner Books rubric emulate the signal traits of *Green Eggs and Ham*: tightly executed plots, strict correspondence between text and illustration, a simple and limited vocabulary, short sentences in rhyme, and no more than one illustration per page. Though educational, these books often do not tell sequential stories but simply present a concept, stage reflexive vignettes, spell out verse rhymes, or enumerate lists of words that rhyme.

These books are as much about words and syntax as about plotted events. The writer Anna Quindlen nicely observed the proximity between Dr. Seuss's words and animated activity that takes place on his pages when she pointed out that he turns words into "balloon animals." She glosses the phrase to mean that he "took words and juggled and bounced them off the page," and that in so doing he taught "children how language works by playing with it and experimenting with language rules." In his Beginner Books Dr. Seuss constructed comic devices that turned words into sources of pleasure.[26]

The following passage displays several language games—internal rhyme, onomatopoeia, assonance, consonance, alliteration—in which Dr. Seuss separates words from their normal function of making meaning and gives them over to linguistic fun:

> The spots on a Glotz
> are about the same size
> as the dots on a Klotz
> so you first have to spot
> who the one with the dots is.[27]

Like "Moose juice is not goose juice; It's juice for the moose" in *Oh Say Can You Say?* or "I can't blab such blibber blubber.

/ My tongue isn't made of rubber" in *The Fox in Socks*, this tongue twister is enjoyably difficult to pronounce aloud. Additional pleasure results from the ways the words in these phrases wander away from the sense that they also delightfully restore. In these verses Dr. Seuss introduces and intensifies the unresolved tension between the presence and absence of meaning.

In his effort to engage six-year-olds' abbreviated attention spans and limited reading abilities, Dr. Seuss designed titillating linguistic games to capture their interest. The title of *One fish two fish red fish blue fish* switches from numbers to colors as more or less interchangeable ways of keeping track of fish. The juxtaposition of the bones in *fishbones*, *wishbones*, and *trombones* demonstrates how language can be an occasion for verbal entertainment as well as extralinguistic meaning. Although punctuation and syntax are necessary to provide order to a sentence, they too can become playthings. A Juggling Jott who plays with punctuation, not letters, can

> juggle some stuff
> You might think he could not . . .
> Such as twenty-two question marks,
> Which is a lot.

Also forty-four commas
And, *also*, one dot![28]

In *On Beyond Zebra!* Dr. Seuss shows how the invention of a new language can help him dream up new worlds. When he frees letters and punctuation from practical obligations, he demonstrates how the alphabet itself is the outcome of revisable conventions. Beginner Books also indicate the relationship between pictures and text, showing that print is not part of the picture, but a caption crucial to understanding what is going on in the image. The text of *I Can Read with My Eyes Shut!* includes the passage:

If you read with your eyes shut
you're likely to find
that the place where you're going
is far, far behind.[29]

The picture accompanying the text exhibits a cat driving a car through a confusing set of roads with signs pointing to such mythical places as Omsk, Oz, and XYZ.

BEFORE THE BEGINNING: BRIGHT AND EARLY BOOKS

Beginner Books became so popular that Random House executives decided to expand the market to include a series called Bright and Early Books that would instruct preschool children in how to read. Random House described the books in Dr. Seuss's Bright and Early series as "an attempt to initiate very young children into the mysteries of reading by seeing to it that almost every word in the text is neatly juxtaposed with an illustration of the object it describes." In its promotion of the series Random House bragged that this modification of Beginner Books "will send a child to first grade with a knowledge of most of the words he'll learn in the first grade."[30]

The books in this series are modeled after *Hop on Pop*, which does not tell a story but simply presents a concept. Designed for a beginning reader, the words in these books are printed in large type, and they are bound in octavo- rather than quarto-size format. Because there are sometimes two pictures to a page, they do not take place against a fully developed background. *Hop on Pop* is the simplest Seuss for youngest use, its brevity accommodating its readers' shorter attention span. Titles such as *Mr. Brown Can Moo! Can You?* invite the readers' participation. The emphasis in books like *The Shape of Me and Other Stuff* is on simple concepts—feet, eyes, shapes—and words that children can readily learn. Stopping in the middle of one of these books does not necessarily interrupt the flow.

What Has Happened to Us?

In 1964 *Business Week* estimated royalties from the sales of Dr. Seuss books at $200,000 a year. In 1967 five Beginner Books—Helen's children—were included on the list of the top fifteen best-selling children's books. *Green Eggs and Ham* stood at the top of the list. Except for *The Seven Lady Godivas* and *The Cat in the Hat Songbook*, the sales of all of Dr. Seuss's children's books increased as a consequence of the success of the Beginner Books enterprise.

From the moment of their initial encounter at Oxford in 1926, Helen had been an indispensable part of Geisel's life, career, and creative process. After their marriage in 1927 she supported them by teaching English before he landed a job with *Judge*, and throughout their marriage she maintained the budget, the household, and Ted's schedule. The spectacular disarray Peter T. Hooper made in his absent mother's kitchen while preparing a batch of Scrambled Eggs Super-Dee-Dooper-dee-Booper in *Scrambled Eggs Super* reveals what probably would have happened to the Geisels' household had Helen left it in her husband's hands. When she first became ill in 1953 Geisel asked his niece, Peggy, who had moved out of the tower studio after she married Alfred Owens in 1952, to move back in and help take care of the household.[31] Without his wife Ted felt more helpless than the small children about whom he wrote. The opening lines of "Prayer for a Child," which he published in *Collier's* magazine in December 1955, give some indication of his state of mind:

From here on earth,
From my small place
I ask of You
Way out in space.[32]

Geisel dedicated his 1955 book *On Beyond Zebra!* to Helen. He began work on the book while she was recovering her ability to walk. In writing it he performed a kind of magical thinking. The couple always knew it was time to take a trip when either one of them felt stuck in some kind of mental or physical slump. *On Beyond Zebra!* described places and creatures that lay beyond the known alphabet. The promise of going to uncharted, previously unimaginable places was Geisel's way of exhorting Helen to get back on her feet. *On Beyond Zebra!* also created an alternative world into which Geisel could escape were Helen to die.

In 1964 the symptoms associated with Guillain-Barré syndrome returned. Helen frequently lost her balance, felt a growing paralysis in her legs, and feared that she might be going blind. Although terrified of losing her, Geisel believed that to survive he needed to distance himself from her. At sixty Ted believed that he had at least another twenty years of productive work.[33]

Some friends explained his growing disaffection as the result of Helen's having become overly protective in ways that impeded his creativity. His juvenile editor Walter Retan described the tension he sensed: "They had so much in common, but they were driving each other crazy. Helen wasn't well, and she probably depressed Ted. She had been very, very good for him, but I could not say she was good for him at that time." Bob Bernstein recalled a conversation in which Geisel complained that he was finding it hard to work in the tower and that he was "considering leasing a studio."[34]

The need to separate from Helen impelled Geisel to repeat the quest for a substitute family that he had embarked upon four decades earlier. Following the return of Helen's illness in 1964, he began to transfer his primary sense of belonging onto another family. That family was composed of Audrey Stone Dimond, who was then married to the chief cardiologist at Scripps Hospital, Grey Dimond, and her daughters, Lark and Lea. The Dimonds moved in the same social circles as the Geisels and they enjoyed each other's company. In 1965 he dedicated the Beginner Book *Fox in Socks* to Audrey of the "Mt. Soledad Lingual Laboratory." The next year he dedicated *The Cat and the Hat Songbook* to her two daughters, "Lea and Lark of Ludington Lane." Geisel's relationship with Audrey soon replaced his relationship with Helen as his primary emotional attachment.

Geisel's collaborator, the animator Chuck Jones, interpreted the romance with Audrey as a rebellion against Helen's disciplinary attitude: "As one side went to gray the other side came into the sunlight. . . . Audrey came along and she was vital and pretty and young and had a wonderful charm about her."[35] Audrey was in many ways Helen's antithesis. Rather than playing the role of artistic collaborator, Audrey enjoyed pointing out that she had never heard of Dr. Seuss until she moved to La Jolla. When she was first introduced to Dr. Seuss, Audrey is reputed to have mistaken him for an ear, nose, and throat specialist and inquired whether he was better known for his work on the right nostril or the left. Geisel's official biographers, Judith and Neil Morgan, have written what is perhaps the most perceptive commentary on the sources of Geisel's attraction to Audrey. They compared her with Marnie, his first playmate. But they also spelled out qualities that Helen and Audrey (and Marnie) shared:

> The women who grew close to Ted throughout his life tended to watch over him in ways that roused their instincts as mother or lover, and sometimes both. With men he laughed, sang, drank and bantered, but with women he admired he always seemed on a first date. They considered him an unordinary mortal, a trusting and needful man who craved their understanding and approval. Some saw him as a gallant child-man full of wit and passion, and found themselves seeking to shelter and insulate him from the world he never entirely confronted.[36]

Helen's symptoms continued to worsen, and she became depressed about Geisel's new relationship. On October 23, 1967, the Geisel's housekeeper Alberta Shaw arrived at the tower to find that Helen had committed suicide the night before. The note she wrote on the stationery of the La Jolla Beach and Tennis Club read in part:

Dear Ted,

What has happened to us?

I don't know.

I feel myself in a spiral going down down down, into a black hole from which there is no escape, no brightness. And loud in my ears from every side I hear, "failure, failure, failure. . . ."

I love you so much. . . . I am too old and enmeshed in everything you do and are, that I cannot conceive of life without you. . . . My going will leave quite a rumor but you can say I was overworked and overwrought. Your reputation with your fans will not be harmed. . . . Sometimes think of the fun we had all thru the years.[37]

Dr. Seuss's Legacy

After reading Helen's suicide note, Ted reportedly said that he didn't know whether he should kill himself or burn down the house.[1] He titled the first book he published after Helen's death *The Foot Book*. This pre–Beginner Book was about how to put one foot in front of the other. It began "Left foot Right foot."

It took several days before Geisel was finally able to talk with Peggy about the fact that Helen had committed suicide. "He was in anguish," Peggy later told Geisel's biographers. "I think he was trying to protect me. . . . Whatever Helen did, she did it out of absolute love for Ted."[2] Having talked over Helen's suicide with Peggy, he was next confronted with the task of explaining his decision to marry Audrey to the representative member of his extended family, Donald Bartlett.

> I've written you kids at least ten times about my future plans,
> And, everytime, torn the letters up. The letters get so involved

so unbelievable. So let me put it out, flat on the line, without any comment or begging for understanding. On the 21st of June, Audrey Dimond is going to Reno to divorce Grey Dimond. . . . Audrey and I are going to be married about the first week of August. I am acquiring two daughters, aged nine and fourteen. I am rebuilding the house to take care of the influx. I am sixty-four years old, I am marrying a woman eighteen years younger. . . . I have not flipped my lid. This is not a sudden nutty decision. . . . This is an inevitable, inescapable conclusion to five years of four people's frustration. All I ask you is to try to believe me.[3]

They were married on August 8, 1968, a week before Audrey's forty-seventh birthday, in a marriage ceremony to which they invited no friends. In September Audrey accompanied Geisel on a trip to Springfield to help his father move into a nursing home. T. R. died four months later, on December 9, 1968, at the age of eighty-nine.

Geisel published more than twenty books from the time of Helen's death in 1967 until his own in 1991. But he now addressed these books to two audiences. In addition to educating new readers, he appealed to the adults who read the books to their children. Unable to decide whether he was writing adult books for children or children's books for adults, Geisel rationalized this indecision with the observation, "The kids I first wrote for . . . are not old poops yet but they have their feet in the door."[4]

Audrey supplied the inspiration for this change in the direction of his imaginative attention when she told him he was writing for humanity, not just for children. She also advised him to change from primary colors to pastels. Having grown up a second time from within the children's books he created, Dr. Seuss stopped writing children's books addressed solely to children and began writing primers for adults. In so doing he turned the child's world in the direction of adults and initiated a conversation across generations.

Dr. Seuss represented this shift in focus most clearly in *Did I Ever Tell You How Lucky You Are?* (1973), whose child narrator can find his way out of feeling "sour and blue" only by recalling lines from the song an old man sang to him one day in "the Desert of Drize." This young boy significantly differs from the descendants of Marco from *Mulberry Street*. Whereas Marco's gang enter fantastical topographies liberated from adult supervision, this young boy finds comfort in the old man's counsel that no matter how terrible his troubles might appear, there are others "muchly much-much more unlucky" than he. The old man's wisdom recalls the lesson the child had to learn on his own in *I Had Trouble in Getting to Solla Sollew*. That boy, who wanted to be free of his day-to-day problems, sought refuge in the delusory Solla Sollew, "where they never have troubles, at least very few." He could have saved himself the trip had he heard the old man's lesson in the Desert of Drize: take what life sends your way and "thank goodness you're not something someone forgot."[5]

This adult orientation also resulted in books with themes concerned with the care of the self. Some reflected on activities that Geisel associated with the creative process, such as drawing (*I Can Draw It Myself by Me Myself with a Little Help from My Friend Dr. Seuss*, 1970), sleeping, dreaming, thinking (*Oh, the Thinks You Can Think!* 1975), and talking (*Oh Say Can You Say?* 1975). *Hunches in Bunches* (1982) concludes with a "hunch" that brings the young protagonist's physical appetites into harmony with his unfleshly ambitions: After determining "the best hunch of the bunch! / I followed him into the kitchen / and had six hot dogs for lunch."[6]

Other books are concerned with changes in the body precipitated by aging. Geisel's health was a continual worry. In the 1970s he underwent a series of cataract operations; in 1975 he had a minor heart attack that damaged his heart muscle; and in 1982 a dentist found a lesion on his tongue. He underwent radiation treatment, but the cancer still spread to a lymph node in his neck, which required radical neck dissection and an invasive biopsy. The operations gave Geisel trouble talking. It is difficult to separate the books that deal with body upkeep—*The Shape of Me and Other Stuff* (1973), *I Can Read with My Eyes Shut!* (1978), and *The Tooth Book* (1981)—from Geisel's medical problems in those years.

He wrote *You're Only Old Once*, which was published on his eighty-second birthday, March 2, 1986, after becoming fed up with this seemingly endless round of medical procedures. He dedicated the book with "affection and affliction" to his surviving classmates from the Dartmouth class of 1925, as a book written for "obsolete children."[7] The Book of the Month Club advertised it as meant for "children 95 years and younger."

Two of the six Big Books he wrote during his twenty-three years of marriage to Audrey engaged Big Issues. *The Lorax* and *The Butter Battle Book* took as their subjects the pollution of the environment and the proliferation of nuclear weapons. These books also introduced changes in the structure and form of his writing.

The children's literature scholar Selma Lanes points out the following characteristics in Dr. Seuss's books: "The action of all his books with children as protagonists take place either (1) in the absence of grownups, or (2) in the imagination."[8] But *The Lorax, The Butter Battle Book,* and *Oh, the Places You'll Go!* represent an adult instructing a child in how and what to inherit from the adult's generation. All of these adult figures want to pass something on. They are liminal figures in that they do not belong to a present or a past and they cannot quite be included in the social order of which they are a part.

THE LORAX

Audrey's care of Geisel's health helped him get through sick spells that might have otherwise crushed his spirit. There is no doubt that she gave him new vitality. Geisel's dedication of *I Can Lick Thirty Tigers Today* to her in 1969 is one index of how well her influence was taking hold. After his first cataract operation she also persuaded him to use softer hues in addition to primary colors. Dr. Seuss's palette now included mauve, plum purple, and sage green. Audrey proved herself even better at handling business matters than Helen. Under her supervision Dr. Seuss Enterprises, which she founded in 1993, grew into an extremely successful business.

When Geisel became exceedingly stressed while working on *The Lorax* in 1970, Audrey took him on a trip to Africa. During their stay at the Mt. Safari Hotel he watched a herd of elephants walk across the mountain, then wrote, "I don't know how it happened but the logjam broke, I had nothing but a laundry list with me, and I grabbed it, I wrote 90% of the book that afternoon." It was at the same hotel that Geisel first imagined the "shortish and oldish and brownish and mossy character" who "spoke with a voice that was sharpish and bossy." Geisel decided the character would be named a Lorax: "I looked at the drawing board and that's what he was!"[9]

The Lorax opens with a conversation between a child and an adult figure called the Once-ler who resides in a ramshackle house on the outskirts of town where only grickle grass can grow. The child visits the Once-ler to hear about the legendary figure called the Lorax. The Once-ler was a pioneer whose travels ended when he arrived at a natural paradise full of beautiful Truffula trees. Discovering that he can turn the tufts of the trees into yarn, he begins to harvest all the trees in order to make a shapeless, useless garment called a thneed.

After the Once-ler cuts down the first Truffula tree, the Lorax emerges from its stump to protest against his further tampering with the trees and wildlife. But the lure of money induces the Once-ler to call all of his relatives to manufacture thneeds in a factory that pollutes the air and water. Rather than paying heed to the Lorax's protest, the Once-ler informs him:

> I'm figgering on biggering
> And BIGGERING
> And BIGGERING
> and BIGGERING
> turning MORE Truffula Trees into thneeds
> Which everyone, EVERYONE, *EVERYONE* needs![10]

The Lorax calls the Once-ler crazy with greed and speaks on behalf of the rights of the Barbaloots and the fish and the swans to have clean water and clean air. But the Once-ler is dedicated to business, and "business must grow," so he does not listen to the dire predictions. Finally, when the last tree is cut down, the

Lorax disappears into the air, leaving a stone marker cryptically inscribed "Unless,"

> where the Lorax once stood
> just as long as it could
> before somebody lifted the Lorax away.

The Once-ler's vocal eccentricities and apparel—the snergedly hose, the gruvvulous glove, and miff-muffed moof—exemplify symptoms of the ecological disaster he has wrought. Besides his eyes, the only parts of his body that are visible to the boy are the hands that once wielded the super axe hacker to fell the Truffula trees.

The communication between the Once-ler and the child is the reverse of the Once-ler's former conversation with the Lorax. The Once-ler now speaks for the Lorax just as the Lorax had formerly spoken on behalf of the trees (who "have no tongues") and the creatures who lost their natural habitat as a consequence of the Once-ler's greed. As the survivor of his rapacious greed, the Once-ler attests to the devastating effects of his actions on "human nature." Remaining as witness to the disastrous consequences of his own greed, the Once-ler speaks *as* the voice of the absent Lorax.

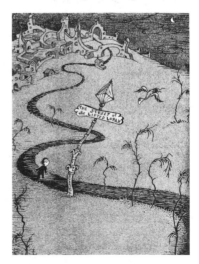

After the Once-ler produces the desire in his young listener to bring about the return of the Lorax, he explains how to go about fulfilling this desire. He gives him a Truffula

seed, whose development requires his daily care. The Once-ler instructs the boy to "give it clean water" and fresh air because the Lorax and his friends will not come back "UNLESS someone like you / cares a whole awful lot."

After Random House distributed *The Lorax* to bookstores in 1971 *Newsweek* called it a hard-sell ecological allegory. Some of Dr. Seuss's most loyal fans expressed their disappointment at the way the tale's message supplanted Dr. Seuss's zaniness for its own sake. The book did not get onto the best-seller lists until the environmental movement picked it up.[11]

DR. SEUSS'S LEGACY

Environmental activists were not the first to adopt a Dr. Seuss book for political aims, and they would not be the last. Dr. Seuss was considered the poet laureate of the baby boomer generation. Characters like the Grinch and the Cat in the Hat and Seussian expressions such as "A person's a person no matter how small" entered the vernacular. Teachers, ministers, businessmen, and propagandists had also taken to adapting his words to their agendas. Politicians were especially adept at conscripting Seussian figures to authorize their political allegories. Having worked in advertising, Geisel considered these adaptations a form of publicity.

Most of it was welcome publicity, though there were some exceptions. Antiabortion advocates adopted Horton's "A person's a person no matter how small" as their slogan and refused to remove the phrase until threatened with legal action. Geisel also used the law to protect the Dr. Seuss name from degrading publicity. Citing a professional embarrassment, he sued to prevent the republication of a forty-year-old drawing from *Liberty*, and he blocked production of Dr. Seuss dolls.[12]

The *Washington Post* columnist Art Buchwald brought Dr. Seuss's political standing to another level when he asked for permission to use the rhythm and phrases from *Marvin K. Mooney Won't You Go Now!* in a column beseeching President Richard M. Nixon to get out of office:

Richard M. Nixon will you please go now
The time has come
The time is now
Just go
Go
Go![13]

President Nixon resigned eight days later, on August 8, 1974, and Geisel wrote Buchwald, "We should have collaborated sooner."[14]

In 1977 he accompanied Kenneth Montgomery, the man who had initiated him fifty years earlier into the most exclusive of Dartmouth's senior societies, to deliver the commencement address and receive an honorary degree at Lake Forest College, where Montgomery was a trustee. The knight voted least likely to succeed delivered what he proudly described as "the briefest Commencement talk ever delivered." Geisel, who had been

writing and rewriting it for over a year, entitled the speech, which
took seventy-five seconds to recite, "My Uncle Terwilliger and
the Art of Eating Popovers":

> My uncle ordered popovers
> From the restaurant's bill of fare.
> And when they were served,
> He regarded them
> With a penetrating stare . . . .
> Then he spoke great Words of Wisdom
> As he sat there on that chair:
> "To eat these things,"
> said my uncle,
> "you must exercise great care.
> You may swallow down what's solid. . .
> BUT . . .
>> You *must* spit out the air!"
>
> And . . .
> As *you* partake of the world's bill of fare,
> That's darned good advice to follow.
> Do a lot of spitting out the hot air.
> And be careful what you swallow.[15]

Throughout the last sixteen years of his life Geisel gathered
reference sources for what he described as his nonautobiography. In 1986 he began a series of interviews with Judith and Neil
Morgan, and arrangements were made for his papers to be
deposited at the Geisel Memorial Library at the University of
California, San Diego.

He also began rereading his earlier children's books for signs
of the negative stereotyping that he had condemned in his 1952

essay on conditioned humor. He removed the image of the yellow-faced and pig-tailed "Chinaman who eats with sticks" in *And to Think That I Saw It on Mulberry Street* and in its place put "Chinese man who eats with sticks." Despite pressure from feminist critics who found it offensive, however, he refused to remove the line "Even Jane could think of that" from Marco's monologue. He reasoned, "[That line] remains in my book because that's what the boy said." Because he took pride in having invented imaginary creatures that he believed were at once asexual and free of ethnicity, he found the accusation of sexism in Alison Lurie's 1990 essay on his writings in the *New York Review of Books* especially insulting: Most characters were animals "and if she can identify their sex, I'll remember her in my will."[16]

In 1985 an article appeared in *Publishers Weekly* titled "Look Who Just Turned Thirty—The Cat in the Hat." Princeton University's class of 1985 awarded him an honorary degree. He won an Emmy for the children's television special *The Grinch Grinches the Cat in the Hat* and a Pulitzer Prize "for his contribution over nearly half a century to the education and enjoyment of America's children and their parents."

In 1988 Random House bought out Vanguard books and reprinted *Mulberry Street* and *The 500 Hats* under the Random imprint. By this time author royalties from the sale of Dr. Seuss books were close to two million dollars a year, and deferred income from Beginner Books that accumulated in trust funds was estimated at more than five million dollars. In 1990 *Publishers Weekly* estimated that Dr. Seuss had sold more children's books in America, and made more money doing so, than any other author.

The madness of taking up intractable positions was one of his favorite topics for the books that Dr. Seuss wrote during the cold war. This theme drove the plot of "The Zax," a story collected in the volume *The Sneetches and Other Stories* that he published in 1961, during the heyday of nuclear proliferation. That narrative turned around the refusal of the North-Going Zax to get out of way of the South-Going Zax, and vice versa. The story concluded with the building of a highway over the Zax that left them standing unbudged in their tracks. In 1981 he decided to address the question of the arms race, which had escalated under President Ronald Reagan, head-on: "I'm not anti-military . . . . I'm just anti-crazy. We did the same things in WWI and WWII. Why can't we learn?"[17] So he wrote a book in which Yooks and Zooks, who are separated from one another by a Berlin-like wall, build increasingly destructive weapons with which they threaten to destroy one another's civilizations. The book ends inconclusively with a little boy running to see whether

or not his grandfather will drop a nuclear device dubbed the "Bitsy Big-Boy Boomeroo" on the Zooks, who threaten to destroy the Yooks with the same weapon.

His editors at Random House told Geisel that children would get freaked out by the inconclusive ending of *The Butter Battle Book*. A copy reader urged him to write an ending that would reassure children that the Yooks and Zooks would not destroy each other, "an illusion that I think children are entitled to." They wanted to change the title to *The Yooks and the Zooks*. But after Audrey intervened on Ted's behalf, the editors restored the original title. He dedicated *The Butter Battle Book* "to Audrey with love." It was published on March 2, 1984, his eightieth birthday.

The book describes a prolonged war between the Yooks and Zooks, which are human-looking animals with balding heads and beaks. The story is told by the child protagonist in the form of a dialogue with his grandfather: "On the last day of summer, /ten hours before Fall . . . / . . . my grandfather took me out to the Wall."[18] But most of the space is devoted to the grandfather's narration of the history of the hostility between the Yooks and the Zooks, which he believes will arrive at its culmination on this particular day: "You will see me make History / RIGHT HERE AND RIGHT NOW."

The issue that divides the two cultures is whether it is appropriate to butter one's bread on the top side, where the Yooks believe their butter should go, or on the bottom side, the way the Zooks do it. The grandfather believes he must inculcate the proper understanding in his grandson, so he informs him that it's high time that he knew

Of the terribly horrible things that the Zooks do
In every Zook house and in every Zook town
Every Zook eats his bread with the butter side down!

The issue of buttering bread becomes one of national pride and honor to be fought to the death. The wall separating the two cultures gradually escalates into a higher and higher wall with border patrols. As it grows in size, the Yooks who live in peaceful coexistence with the Zooks become increasingly militant, with brass bands and increasingly sophisticated weaponry spurring them on. The ultimate weapon is Bitsy Big-Boy Boomeroo, a small pellet of which has the capacity to blow up the Zooks and the Yooks.

At the conclusion of the tale the boy watches helplessly as his grandfather picks up his Bitsy Big-Boy to engage his Zook counterpart in a game of nuclear brinkmanship on the wall. The tale ends with the boy looking on as his grandfather and the old man's Zook alter ego stare each other down, each poised to drop the Boomeroo:

"Who's going to drop it?
Will you . . . ? Or will he . . . ?"
"Be patient," said grandpa. "We'll see.
We will see . . ."

The grandfather wants the boy to wait with the other Zooks in an underground bunker while he makes history by winning the war: "You should be down in that hole! / And you're up here instead!" The grandfather nonetheless wants his grandson to be the witness to the history he believes he is making. But instead of identifying with the grandfather's animosity, the grandson shouts, "Be careful! Oh, gee!"

The child sees what the reader sees, namely, that the situation his grandfather wants him to inherit is hopeless. The art of the story turns on Dr. Seuss's representation of the difference in the time orientations of the grandfather and his grandson. The grandson recounts his grandfather's story as if it took place in the past, "ten hours before Fall." The sense of imminent war is part of the grandfather's history rather than the grandson's reality. The grandson is recollecting events that have happened rather than reporting them as they occur. The events that take place in the child's account happened in his past and can be resurrected only if the reader chooses to identify with the grandfather's hostility. The blank page with which the book concludes is not an open ending; it is the site where a new history can begin after the child turns the page on the grandfather's history.

Maurice Sendak wrote the following blurb for the book: "Surprisingly, wonderfully, the case for total disarmament has been brilliantly made by our acknowledged master of nonsense, Dr. Seuss. . . . Only a genius of the ridiculous could possibly deal with the cosmic and lethal madness of the nuclear arms race. . . . He has done the world a service." Buchwald said Geisel should have a Nobel Prize. The *Kirkus* reviewer was more critical, calling the book "a little out-of-date, even a little out-of-keeping." Charles Osgood of *CBS News* reported, "*The Butter Battle Book* of Dr. Seuss / Is much too much like the Evening Neuss." Nevertheless the book was translated into more languages than any other Dr. Seuss book, and it sold heavily in Britain. On New Year's Day of 1990 *The Butter Battle Book* was televised across Russia. "Right after that, the USSR began falling apart," Geisel mused.[19]

In 1986, for the first time since his father's death twenty years earlier, Geisel decided to visit Springfield, Massachusetts. The day he arrived the townspeople lined the streets to turn the parade that Marco had imagined into a reality. Fifty years after he had begun work on *And to Think That I Saw It on Mulberry Street* children held up signs saying "And to Think That I Saw *Him* on Mulberry Street."

Geisel had become Springfield's favorite son. An iconic figure whose works had sold millions of copies and been translated into fifteen languages, Dr. Seuss eradicated the memories of the derision his family experienced during World War I. Rather than depend on the townspeople's approbation, however, Dr. Seuss elevated Springfield's ranking. The mayor took children through what he described as Dr. Seuss's father's park and picked up a sign that read "Geisel Grove." When he visited his boyhood home on 74 Fairfield Street, Geisel told the little boy who now lived there where to find the doodles that he had drawn on the wallpaper seventy years earlier.

After the tour Geisel reportedly told Audrey, "As far as this town is concerned, I am already dead." Despite the passage of time and the salutary powers of Dr. Seuss's art, however, he never forgot the public humiliation he had experienced as a young boy. "I can visualize," he wrote Chuck Jones in 1987, "these poor kids being chased home from school, being clobbered . . . with bric bats in the same way I was when I was a kid with a German father. When they clobbered me, they yelled 'Kill the Kaiser!' "[20]

METICULOSITY

Geisel's management of his legacy during this period included giving numerous interviews about how he made his children's books. These interviews invariably included cautionary remarks about the amount of time writers should devote to their craft each day. In 1974 he supplied the actor and producer Jack Webb with the following detailed description of his work process:

> I've made it a rule to sit at my desk for eight hours even if nothing comes, I've seen so many writers and artists become bums especially in a resort town like this. They go to the beach in the morning and when they come back they don't feel like working. So I work eight hours straight. When the work is going well, I'll go at it hammer and tongs for a month, then take six or seven months off. Even then I'll be working, though, filling up notebooks with ideas.[21]

He often threw away two hundred pages of verse before he settled on one "finished" stanza.

The poet Karla Kuskin once said that she thought his creatures all had "slightly batty oval eyes and a smile that you might find on a Mona Lisa after her first martini."[22] Geisel was fond of quoting Kuskin's description as a prelude to his own explanation of the Seussian method of drawing: "Since I can't draw, I've taken the awkwardness and peculiarities of my natural style and developed them. That's why my characters look that way. . . . Kids exaggerate the same way I do. They overlook things they can't draw. Their pencil slips and they get funny effects. I've learned to incorporate my pencil slips into my style."[23] Janet Schulman, who worked with him as one of his editors at Random House, described his work process as an art of transition: "When he was working on a book, he always had a general idea of what the book was going to be. But he put these pieces of paper on the wall and there would be holes within each sequences that usually belonged to the transition points."[24]

His drawings underwent even more revisions than his verse copy. In a public conversation that he held with the children's book author Maurice Sendak in 1989 he described the key to his productivity as "meticulosity."[25] Dr. Seuss painstakingly drew and redrew the illustrations that accompanied his verse fantasies until they seemed as streamlined and concise as his verse copy.

After watching Dr. Seuss put together a panel for one of his illustrated books, the editor Michael Frith was inspired to provide this account:

> To watch him at work is to watch a man in perpetual motion: his hand plunges into one of the myriad pots of colored pencils that surround him, selects one, sketches fiercely and whips the drawing off its pad. In two strides he is at the wall, push-pins plunge, and picture affixed, he considers it for an intense moment with eyebrows cocked in concentration. Then he is back at his desk, trying variation after variation until he has the one that satisfies him.[26]

OH, THE PLACES YOU'LL GO!

In 1989 his doctors informed Geisel that cancer had spread to his bone marrow, and he began work on what he knew would be his final book. The title recalled Geisel to his first prolonged adventure away from home. When he was a freshman at Dartmouth, the phrase "Oh, the places you'll go!" served as the verbal equivalent to a handshake. After being pronounced by one student, it immediately evoked the response "The people you'll meet!"

Following its publication in 1990 *Oh, the Places You'll Go!* quickly entered the *New York Times* best-seller list as the ideal graduation gift. It remained on the list for two years and sold more than 1.5 million copies. Valedictory in its form as well as subject matter, the book includes scenes and characters from *Horton Hears a Who*, *The Cat in the Hat*, *The Sneetches*, *The Lorax*, *I Had Trouble in Getting to Solla Sollew*, *The Butter Battle Book*, *Empty Pants*, *Green Eggs and Ham*, *If I Ran the Zoo*, and other Seussiana that changed the cartography of children's literature.

It also includes figures—the hippocrass, the flying cow, the goat whose milk sold for an inflated price—that first appeared in the *Jack-O-Lantern* and *Judge*. Although it repeats the journey format of *I Had Trouble Getting to Solla Sollew*, it turns the process of journeying into an end in itself. Every locale through which the child passes, even the seemingly dreadful "waiting place," becomes the occasion for him to discover that "Life's a Great Balancing Act" if you never forget the difference between your right foot and your left.

The book brings Dr. Seuss's career full circle by linking the child's journey with the child narrator's point of departure in *And to Think That I Saw It on Mulberry Street*. In a sense the adult narrator says what Marco had hoped his father would have said when he left home for school each morning. In Dr. Seuss's earlier tales the adult narrator is an implied presence, but in *Oh, the Places You'll Go!* the adult provides the verbal impetus to carry the child through the visual adventure. What draws children, and readers in general, to this tale is not only the prospect of traveling to fascinating worlds, but the promise of Dr. Seuss's company.

Oh, the Places You'll Go! is structured as an intergenerational dialogue. It follows the trajectory of a child about to set out on a life journey that will expose him to sights and spectacles even more wondrous than Marco encountered in his trip along Mulberry Street. But unlike Marco, this child draws the motivation for his travel from the voice of the narrator's extravagantly enthusiastic exhortations: "Oh, the places you'll go! Kid You'll move mountains!" Inextricably connected with the child whose ambitions he inspires, the adult narrator is also saying farewell to the child within. The overarching categorical imperative for the child's journey is "We can and we must do better than this!," the phrase Geisel told Judith and Neil Morgan he wanted to be remembered as his last words.

When it was published in 1990 *Oh, the Places You'll Go!* was interpreted as a valedictory address: Geisel's effort to say farewell with a flourish. But he did not in fact say farewell until he asked his stepdaughter Lea Grey to take Theophrastus, the ragged brown toy dog that he had kept near his work table since childhood: "You will take care of the dog won't you?"[27]

Sometime around 10 p.m. on September 24, 1991, Theodor Seuss Geisel died in his sleep next to the drawing board on which he created the figures that have changed the ways children—and adults—dream.

Acknowledgments

I FIRST BEGAN THINKING ABOUT THIS BOOK IN 1990. AFTER BEING awarded the Ted and Helen Geisel Third Century Professorship in the Humanities that year, I felt a certain indebtedness to the benefactor. Adam Lipisus intensified my resolve to write this book when he began research on Theodor Geisel's career at Dartmouth, which he turned into a splendid senior thesis entitled *The Birth of Dr. Seuss* in 1994.

I have incurred even more debts to numerous colleagues and friends for their advice and help. For individual research assistance I would like to thank Wole Ojurongbe of the Dartmouth Master of Arts in Liberal Studies Program, my Presidential scholar Karen Iorio, and Jay Satterfield and Joshua D. Shaw of the Rauner Alumni Library. I am grateful to Jeffrey Horrell and Robert Donin for their timely advice about how to get permission to reprint some of Geisel's early work on the *Jack-O-Lantern,* and to Philip Nel and Charles Cohen as well as Herb Cheyette for their guidance in getting the permissions.

I was also blessed with extremely helpful advice from the three editors—Cybele Tom, Timothy Bent, and Dayne Poshusta —with whom I was privileged to work at Oxford University Press. I also thank Judith Hoover for her superb copyediting.

From the very beginning of this project Edward Connery Lathem provided indispensable advice. Ed patiently engaged with every turn in my thinking about Dr. Seuss. He praised what he liked, criticized what he found wrongheaded, told me where to find things when I could not, and gave me facts about which I would not have known to ask. I wish he had lived to see the final version of the manuscript.

Finally, I would like to thank Patricia McKee, who listened this book into existence.

NOTES

1. Judith Morgan and Neil Morgan, *Dr. Seuss and Mr. Geisel: A Biography* (New York: Random House, 1995), 15. They cite this passage from Geisel's unpublished "nonautobiography."
2. From the papers collected in the Dr. Seuss holdings at the University of California at Los Angeles Library.
3. These lines are quoted by Judith Morgan and Neil Morgan from their interview with Geisel. See *Dr. Seuss and Mr. Geisel*, 80–81.
4. Ibid., 13. I have drawn the biographical data primarily from the Morgans' official biography and Charles Cohen, *The Seuss, the Whole Seuss and Nothing but the Seuss: A Visual Biography of Theodor Seuss Geisel* (New York: Random House, 2004). Mary Galbraith also observes the influence of Geisel's 1936 trip to Germany on the composition of the story. But whereas I read Marco's desire to see a circus parade as a sign of his desire to belong to Springfield's civic culture, she sees Marco's exaggerations as complicitous with Hitler's use of parades as a show of German might. See "Agony in the Kindergarten: Indelible German Images in American Picture Books," in *Text, Culture and National Identity in Children's Literature: International Seminar on Children's Literature, Pure and Applied*, ed. Jean Webb (Helsinki: Edita Ltd., 2000), 124–43.
5. Morgan and Morgan, *Dr. Seuss and Mr. Geisel*, 19. The Morgans cite the *Springfield Union* of September 4, 1929, as the source for this statistic.
6. Ibid., 7.
7. Ibid., 6. The Morgans cite Geisel's nonautobiography as the source for this expression.
8. This line appears in Geisel's notes for his seminars and lectures on children's books that he gave at the University of Utah Writing Seminar in 1947. These papers are collected in the Dr. Seuss holdings at the Mandeville Special Collections Library of the Geisel Library at the University of California at San Diego, Box 19, Folder 6.

9. Morgan and Morgan, *Dr. Seuss and Mr. Geisel*, 83.

10. Dr. Seuss, *And to Think That I Saw It on Mulberry Street* (1937; New York: Vanguard, 1964). There are no page numbers in the text.

11. See Jonathan Cott, "The Good Dr. Seuss," in *Of Sneetches and Whos and the Good Dr. Seuss: Essays on the Writing and Life of Theodor Geisel*, ed. Thomas Fensch (Jefferson, NC: McFarland, 1997), 108.

12. Robert Sullivan, "Oh, the Places He Went!" *Dartmouth Alumni Magazine* 84 (Winter 1991): 22.

13. Morgan and Morgan, *Dr. Seuss and Mr. Geisel*, 7. The Morgans cite their interview with Geisel as the source for this recollection.

14. Geisel recited these lines from memory after Jonathan Cott suggested their pertinence to the relationship between Marco and his father in *And to Think That I Saw It on Mulberry Street*. Cott, "The Good Dr. Seuss," 110, 108.

15. Ted expressed his admiration for these creatures, which were created by Palmer Cox, in his interview with Jonathan Cott, "The Good Dr. Seuss," 110.

16. In his conversation with Cott, Ted said the Goops were a little "too moralistic" for him. "But I loved the Brownies." Ibid.

17. Morgan and Morgan, *Dr. Seuss and Mr. Geisel*, 7.

18. "Gay Menagerie of Queer Animals Fills the Apartment of Dr. Seuss," *Springfield Daily News*, November 28, 1937, 5E.

19. Morgan and Morgan, *Dr. Seuss and Mr. Geisel*, 9.

20. Ibid., 287.

21. Marisa Gianetti, "Young Readers Welcome Dr. Seuss Back Home," *Springfield Union*, May 21, 1986, 1.

22. Morgan and Morgan, *Dr. Seuss and Mr. Geisel*, 10.

23. Quoted by Michael J. Bandler, "Portrait of a Man Reading," *Washington Post Book World*, May 7, 1972, 2.

24. Kathleen Kudlinski, *Dr. Seuss: Young Author and Artist* (New York: Aladdin Paperbacks, 2005), 6–9.

25. Cohen, *Seuss, the Whole Seuss and Nothing but the Seuss*, 33.

26. Morgan and Morgan, *Dr. Seuss and Mr. Geisel*, 18.

27. See Thomas Fensch, *The Man Who Was Dr. Seuss: The Life and Work of Theodor Geisel* (Woodlands, TX: New Century Books, 2000), 13.

28. Robert Jennings, "Dr. Seuss: What Am I Doing Here?" *Saturday Evening Post* (October 23, 1965): 106.

29. "When I was young, I used to go to the zoo a lot, and when I returned I would try to draw the animals. You see my father, among other things, ran a zoo in Springfield. He was a guy who became president of a Springfield

brewery the day Prohibition was declared (this was wartime prohibition). So he became very cynical and sat for days in the living room saying SOB, SOB over and over—he didn't know what to do with himself." Cott, "Good Dr. Seuss," 110.

30. Morgan and Morgan, *Dr. Seuss and Mr. Geisel*, 23.

31. Ibid., 24.

32. Charles Cohen makes a convincing argument for this source in *Seuss, the Whole Seuss and Nothing but the Seuss*, 17.

33. Ibid., 194.

34. Charles Cohen has traced several changes in the contents of the buggy that the horse pulls. Early in his career with *Judge*, Ted depicted wagons filled with beer kegs. In the ads he composed for the Warren Telechon Clock company, he replaced this image with a consignment of clocks. When he placed an awning over the driver's head he installed flowerpots as his merchandise. See *Seuss, the Whole Seuss and Nothing but the Seuss*, 185.

35. Cohen, *Seuss, the Whole Seuss and Nothing but the Seuss*, 205. After making this observation, Cohen goes on to explain that he can discern no direct causal explanation between Geisel's experiences of stigmatization during his boyhood and his later abhorrence of social injustice. I try to explain what caused Geisel to turn his childhood experiences into the foundation for his vision of social justice in chapter 3 of this book.

36. In a public conversation that he held with Maurice Sendak in 1989, Geisel significantly differentiated the sources of his children's books from Sendak's. "I don't think my childhood influenced my work" in the way Sendak's had. Remarking that he thought he "skipped his childhood" he went on to explain that he viewed his childhood through the lens of the perturbing experiences he underwent in his adolescence. Glenn Edward Sadler, "Maurice Sendak and Dr. Seuss: A Conversation," in *Of Sneetches and Whos and the Good Dr. Seuss: Essays on the Writing and Life of Theodor Geisel*, ed. Thomas Fensch (Jefferson, NC: McFarland, 1997), 138.

TWO

1. See Charles Cohen, *The Seuss, the Whole Seuss and Nothing but the Seuss: A Visual Biography of Theodor Seuss Geisel* (New York: Random House, 2004), 99.

2. Clifton Fadiman, "Books. Or Am I Just Being Cranky?" *New Yorker*, November 6, 1937, 76–80.

3. Beatrix Potter, letter to Anne Carroll Moore, December 18, 1937, in *Beatrix Potter's Americans: Selected Letters*, ed. Jane Crowell Morse (Boston: The Horn Book, 1982), 84.

4. Judith Morgan and Neil Morgan, *Dr. Seuss and Mr. Geisel: A Biography* (New York: Random House, 1995), 83.

5. In *The Seuss, the Whole Seuss and Nothing but the Seuss* Charles Cohen correlates these discrepant figures with Dr. Seuss's art of exaggeration, 183–85.

6. See Tanya Dean, *Theodor Geisel (Dr. Seuss)* (Philadelphia: Chelsea House, 2002), 12.

7. Kathleen Kudlinski, *Dr. Seuss: Young Author and Artist* (New York: Aladdin Paperbacks, 2005), 112–13.

8. Edward Connery Lathem, *The Beginnings of Dr. Seuss: An Informal Reminiscence by Theodor Seuss Geisel: Published in Commemoration of the One-Hundredth Anniversary of His Birth March 2, 1904–2004* (Hanover, NH: Dartmouth College, 2004), 3.

9. Morgan and Morgan, *Dr. Seuss and Mr. Geisel*, 26–39.

10. Ibid., 26.

11. Robert Sullivan, "Oh, the Places He Went!" *Dartmouth Alumni Magazine* 84 (Winter 1991): 24.

12. Morgan and Morgan, *Dr. Seuss and Mr. Geisel*, 37.

13. *The American Press*, 1934. The clipping can be found in the Geisel scrapbook housed in the Dr. Seuss holdings of the Mandeville Special Collections Library in the Geisel Library at the University of California at San Diego, Box 17, Folder 29.

14. Seth Rowland, "Dr. Seuss, Who Entertained Us in Grade School, Gives Us Our Theme for Winter Carnival in Our 'Old Age,'" *The Dartmouth*, February 12, 1981, 8.

15. Morgan and Morgan, *Dr. Seuss and Mr. Geisel*, 36.

16. "The Books That Made Writers," *The Writer* 93, no. 8 (1980): 24.

17. For a fine discussion of Dr. Seuss's drawing style, see Richard Marschall's introduction to *Dr. Seuss: The Tough Coughs as He Ploughs the Dough*, ed. Richard Marschall (New York: William Morrow, 1987), 12.

18. Morgan and Morgan, *Dr. Seuss and Mr. Geisel*, 27.

19. Sullivan, "Oh, the Places He Went!" 24.

20. Charles Cohen uncovers additional May 15s in *If I Ran the Zoo* and *The Seven Lady Godivas* (*Seuss, the Whole Seuss and Nothing but the Seuss*, 68–69).

21. Morgan and Morgan, *Dr. Seuss and Mr. Geisel*, 230.

22. The Morgans cite the letters to Whit Campbell and Robert Sharp in ibid., 33–34.

23. See ibid., 36.

24. The original letter is on deposit in the Dr. Seuss holdings of the Mandeville Special Collections Library in the Geisel Library at the University of California at San Diego, Box 17, Folder 28.

25. Lathem, *Beginnings of Dr. Seuss*, 11.

26. Geisel elaborates on this misunderstanding in ibid., 11–12.

27. See Morgan and Morgan, *Dr. Seuss and Mr. Geisel*, 47–48.

28. See ibid., 45. The Oxford University notebook is on deposit in the Dr. Seuss holdings of the Mandeville Special Collections Library in the Geisel Library at the University of California at San Diego, Box 1, Folder 13.

29. Morgan and Morgan, *Dr. Seuss and Mr. Geisel*, 45.

30. Ibid., 58.

31. Cohen, *Seuss, the Whole Seuss and Nothing but the Seuss*, 73.

32. Lathem, *Beginnings of Dr. Seuss*, 21.

33. Cohen, *Seuss, the Whole Seuss and Nothing but the Seuss*, 74.

34. Morgan and Morgan, *Dr. Seuss and Mr. Geisel*, 62.

35. Robert Jennings, "Dr. Seuss, What Am I Doing Here?" *Saturday Evening Post* (October 23, 1965): 108.

36. Cohen, *Seuss, the Whole Seuss and Nothing but the Seuss*, 79–81.

37. Philip Nel, *Dr. Seuss: American Icon* (New York: Continuum, 2005), 100.

38. Ibid., 206, and Cohen, *Seuss, the Whole Seuss and Nothing but the Seuss*, 307.

39. Cohen, *Seuss, the Whole Seuss and Nothing but the Seuss*, 76–78.

40. Ibid., 76.

41. Ibid., 83.

42. Ibid., 153.

43. Lathem, *Beginnings of Dr. Seuss*, 23.

44. Ibid., 26.

45. Ibid.

46. Cohen, *Seuss, the Whole Seuss and Nothing but the Seuss*, 134.

47. Morgan and Morgan, *Dr. Seuss and Mr. Geisel*, 74–77.

48. Ibid., 73.

49. Cohen, *Seuss, the Whole Seuss and Nothing but the Seuss*, 100, 116–36.

50. Ibid., 104.

51. Ibid., 105.

52. For a representative case of such an interview, see Bob Warren, "Dr. Seuss, Former Jack-O-Lantern Editor, Tells How Boredom May Lead to Success," *The Dartmouth*, May 10, 1934, 9.

53. Cohen, *Seuss, the Whole Seuss and Nothing but the Seuss*, 146–51.

54. Morgan and Morgan, *Dr. Seuss and Mr. Geisel*, 88.

55. Dr. Seuss, *The 500 Hats of Bartholomew Cubbins* (New York: Random House, 1938).

56. Alexander Laing, Review of *The 500 Hats of Bartholomew Cubbins*, *Dartmouth Alumni Magazine*, January 1938, 24.

57. Alexander Laing, cited in the *New York Times Book Review*, July 23, 1939.

58. Theodor Seuss Geisel, letter to Harold Rugg, November 9, 1938, in the Geisel papers collected at the Rauner Library at Dartmouth College.

59. Morgan and Morgan, *Dr. Seuss and Mr. Geisel*, 96.

THREE

1. Judith Morgan and Neil Morgan, *Dr. Seuss and Mr. Geisel: A Biography* (New York: Random House, 1995), 98.

2. Ibid., 97.

3. Ibid.

4. Dr. Seuss, *Horton Hatches the Egg* (New York: Random House, 1940).

5. Charles Cohen, *The Seuss, the Whole Seuss and Nothing but the Seuss: A Visual Biography of Theodor Seuss Geisel* (New York: Random House, 2004), 203.

6. Philip Nel, *Dr. Seuss: American Icon* (New York: Continuum, 2005), 40–41.

7. Richard H. Minear, *Dr. Seuss Goes to War: The World War II Editorial Cartoons of Theodor Seuss Geisel* (New York: New Press, 1999), 38.

8. Morgan and Morgan, *Dr. Seuss and Mr. Geisel*, 102. They cite from Geisel's nonautobiography.

9. Minear, *Dr. Seuss Goes to War*, 28.

10. Ralph Ingersoll, quoted in Andrew Patner, *I. F. Stone: A Portrait* (New York: Pantheon, 1988), 73.

11. Quoted in Morgan and Morgan, *Dr. Seuss and Mr. Geisel*, 101. For an elaboration of Geisel's commitment to *PM*, see Henry Jenkins, " 'No Matter How Small': The Democratic Imagination of Dr. Seuss,' " in *Hop on Pop: The Politics and Pleasures of Popular Culture*, ed. Henry Jenkins, Tara McPherson, and Jane Shattuc (Durham, NC: Duke University Press, 2002), 193. For a contemporary account of Geisel's involvement with *PM*, see "Malice in Wonderland," *Newsweek*, February 9, 1947, 58–59.

12. Max Lerner, preface to Roy Hoopes, *Ralph Ingersoll: A Biography* (New York: Antheneum, 1985), viii.

13. Cohen, *Seuss, the Whole Seuss and Nothing but the Seuss*, 243.

14. Ibid.

15. Ibid., 236–37.

16. Ibid., 205, 241.

17. Minear, *Dr. Seuss Goes to War*, 105.

18. Ibid., 140.

19. Joseph McBride, *Frank Capra: The Catastrophe of Success* (New York: Simon & Schuster, 1992), 453.

20. Cohen, *Seuss, the Whole Seuss and Nothing but the Seuss*, 256.

21. Morgan and Morgan, *Dr. Seuss and Mr. Geisel*, 110.

22. Script from *Your Job in Germany* is deposited in the Dr. Seuss holdings of the Mandeville Special Collections Library in the Geisel Library at the University of California at San Diego, Box 1, Folder 44. This passage is cited in Cohen, *Seuss, the Whole Seuss and Nothing but the Seuss*, 263.

23. Script from *Your Job in Germany*; cited in Morgan and Morgan, *Dr. Seuss and Mr. Geisel*, 111.

24. Morgan and Morgan, *Dr. Seuss and Mr. Geisel*, 111.

25. Ibid., 113.

26. Ibid., 114.

27. Ibid., 116.

28. Henry Jenkins attributed this hope to Dr. Seuss in " 'No Matter How Small,' " 194. See also "Malice in Wonderland," 58–59.

29. T. S. Geisel, Memo to Chief, Special Information Services, December 7, 1944, cited in Jenkins, " 'No Matter How Small,' " 194.

30. T. S. Geisel, Memo to Chief Army Information Branch, I.E.D., February 5, 1945, cited in Jenkins, " 'No Matter How Small,' " 207.

31. Morgan and Morgan, *Dr. Seuss and Mr. Geisel*, 120.

32. Henry Jenkins cited this belief in " 'No Matter How Small,' " 194.

33. Dr. Seuss, Lecture Notes for the University of Utah Workshop, July 1947, are deposited in the Dr. Seuss holdings of the Mandeville Special Collections Library in the Geisel Library at the University of California at San Diego, Box 19, Folder 7, cited in Jenkins, " 'No Matter How Small,' " 194.

34. Ibid., 196, 195.

35. Ibid., 196.

36. Dr. Seuss, Lecture Notes for the University of Utah Workshop, July 1947, Box 19, Folder 7, cited in Morgan and Morgan, *Dr. Seuss and Mr. Geisel*, 124.

37. Mary Dryden interview with Geisel, June 30, 1957, "A Survey of the Popularity and Uses of Dr. Seuss Books in Stimulating Reading Interest and Enjoyment among Children in the Lower Elementary Grades of the Springfield Public Schools" (master's thesis, American International College, Springfield, MA), 28. Her thesis is deposited in the Dr. Seuss Holdings at the University of California at Los Angeles.

38. Robert Jennings, "Dr. Seuss: What Am I Doing Here?" *Saturday Evening Post* (October 23, 1965): 107.

39. Morgan and Morgan, *Dr. Seuss and Mr. Geisel*, 138.

40. Jenkins, " 'No Matter How Small,' " 188.

41. "Writing for Children: A Mission," *Los Angeles Times*, November 27, 1960, 11. The November typescript is deposited in the Dr. Seuss holdings of the Mandeville Special Collections Library in the Geisel Library at the University of California at San Diego, Box 18, Folder 8, cited in Jenkins, " 'No Matter How Small,' " 187. This article also has the title "Brat Books on the March."

42. " . . . But for Grown-Ups Laughing Isn't Any Fun," *New York Times Book Review*, November 16, 1952, 2.

43. Ibid.

44. Dr. Seuss, *On Beyond Zebra!* (New York: Random House, 1956).

45. Dr. Seuss, *Bartholomew and the Oobleck* (New York: Random House, 1949).

46. Dr. Seuss, *Thidwick the Big-Hearted Moose* (New York: Random House, 1948).

47. "Marco Comes Late," *Redbook*, September 1950, 58–59.

48. "How Officer Pat Saved the Whole Town," *Redbook*, October 1950, 46–48.

49. Dr. Seuss, *McElligot's Pool* (New York: Random House, 1947).

50. Dr. Seuss, *If I Ran the Zoo* (New York: Random House, 1950).

51. Dr. Seuss, *If I Ran the Circus* (New York: Random House, 1958).

52. *Gerald McBoing Boing*, directed by Robert Cannon, adapted from a story by Dr. Seuss (by Phil Eastman and Bill Scott) and released by Columbia Pictures, January 25, 1951.

53. Dr. Seuss and Allan Scott, *The 5000 Fingers of Dr. T.*, screenplay, revised final draft, February 25, 1952, 50, cited in Cohen, *Seuss, the Whole Seuss and Nothing but the Seuss*, 289.

54. Morgan and Morgan, *Dr. Seuss and Mr. Geisel*, 138.

55. Ibid., 140.

56. Jenkins, " 'No Matter How Small,' " 195.

57. Morgan and Morgan, *Dr. Seuss and Mr. Geisel*, 137.

58. Ibid.

59. Jenkins, " 'No Matter How Small,' " 188.

60. Jennings, "Dr. Seuss: What Am I Doing Here?" 108.

61. Jenkins, " 'No Matter How Small,' " 187.

62. Dr. Seuss, *Horton Hears a Who* (New York: Random House, 1954).

63. Jenkins, " 'No Matter How Small,' " 187.

64. According to Henry Jenkins, "The child for Seuss was born in an edenic state, outside of adult corruption, yet already possessing, as a birthright, the virtues of a democratic citizen—a sense of fairness and justice, a hunger to belong and participate actively within the community." Ibid., 188. Horton and Jo-Jo regain this Eden.

FOUR

1. Philip Nel, *Dr. Seuss: American Icon* (New York: Continuum, 2005), 24; Philip Nel, *The Annotated Cat: Under the Hats of Dr. Seuss and His Cat* (New York: Random House, 2007), 9–10.

2. Judith Morgan and Neil Morgan, *Dr. Seuss and Mr. Geisel: A Biography* (New York: Random House, 1995), 156.

3. Cited in Nel, *Annotated Cat*, 9–10.

4. John Hersey, "Why Do Students Bog Down after the First R?" *Life*, May 24, 1954, 147–48.

5. Nel, *Annotated Cat*, 8.

6. In *The Uses of Enchantment: The Meaning and Importance of Fairy Tales* (New York: Random House, 1977), Bruno Bettelheim describes how folk tales and fairy tales recuperated the authority of the reality principle through their gratification of the pleasure principle (41–45).

7. Susan Stewart explains how children's literature produces the disjunction between the world as is and the as-if, subjunctive world of alternative realities in *Nonsense: Aspects of Intertextuality in Folklore and Literature* (Baltimore, MD: Johns Hopkins University Press, 1978), 36–38.

8. Dr. Seuss, *The Cat in the Hat* (New York: Random House, 1957).

9. In "Cat People: What Dr. Seuss Really Taught Us," *New Yorker*, December 23 and 30, 2002, 148–54, Louis Menand situates *The Cat in the Hat* in the context of cold war insecurities. He reads the Cat in the Hat as a threatening stranger who undermines and supplants the mother's protective position rather than a substitutive figure through whom the children work through the mother's absence.

10. Geisel's memo to Stanley Kramer about the role dream elements play in Bart's psychic life acquires resonance when associated with Thing One and Thing Two: "The kid, psychologically, is in a box. The dream mechanism takes these elements that are thwarting him and blows them up into gigantic proportions." Cited in Henry Jenkins, " 'No Matter How Small': The Democratic Imagination of Dr. Seuss,' " in *Hop on Pop: The Politics and Pleasures of Popular Culture*, ed. Henry Jenkins, Tara McPherson, and Jane Shattuc (Durham, NC: Duke University Press, 2002), 201.

11. Ruth MacDonald discusses the role the "Bump" plays in drawing the reader's imagination outside the world confined within the children's household in *Dr. Seuss* (Boston: Twayne, 1988), 117. Philip Nel discusses the disparate textual positionings of the Bump in *The Annotated Cat*, 32–38.

12. Philip Nel undertakes a splendid discussion of the role played by these internal rhymes in enabling children to learn how to pronounce a new world in *The Annotated Cat*, 46.

13. Morgan and Morgan, *Dr. Seuss and Mr. Geisel*, 148–49.

14. Edward Connery Lathem, *The Beginnings of Dr. Seuss: An Informal Reminiscence by Theodor Seuss Geisel: Published in Commemoration of the One-Hundredth Anniversary of His Birth March 2, 1904–2004* (Hanover, NH: Dartmouth College, 2004), 35.

15. Edward Martin, "'Dr. Seuss' Has Prolific Pen," *San Diego Union*, August 30, 1953, E2.

16. Helen Palmer Geisel, "1920s Record, 1948–1953," *Wellesley Record Book of 1953* (Wellesley, MA: Wellesley College, 1953), 82.

17. Interview with Robert Bernstein, May 1, 1994, in Adam Lipsius, "The Birth of Dr. Seuss" (senior honors thesis, Dartmouth College, 1994), 132.

18. Morgan and Morgan, *Dr. Seuss and Mr. Geisel*, 157–68, 199.

19. For a discussion of the relationship between Beginner Books and Big Books, see ibid., 169–80.

20. Dr. Seuss, *How the Grinch Stole Christmas!* (New York: Random House, 1957).

21. Dr. Seuss, *Yertle the Turtle and Other Stories* (New York: Random House, 1958).

22. Ruth MacDonald places *The Sneetches and Other Stories* in an antiracist historical context in *Dr. Seuss*, 12. Charles Cohen elaborates on that context in *The Seuss, the Whole Seuss and Nothing but the Seuss: A Visual Biography of Theodor Seuss Geisel* (New York: Random House, 2004), 220–21.

23. Morgan and Morgan, *Dr. Seuss and Mr. Geisel*, 173.

24. Dr. Seuss, *The Sneetches and Other Stories* (New York: Random House, 1961).

25. Dr. Seuss, *Green Eggs and Ham* (New York: Random House, 1960).

26. Anna Qunidlen, "The One Who Had Fun," *New York Times*, September 28, 1991, 19.

27. Dr. Seuss, *Oh Say Can You Say?* (New York: Random House, 1979).

28. Dr. Seuss, *If I Ran the Circus* (New York: Random House, 1958).

29. Dr. Seuss, *I Can Read with My Eyes Shut!* (New York: Random House, 1978).
30. Ruth MacDonald cites this description of Bright and Early Books in *Dr. Seuss*, 140.
31. Morgan and Morgan, *Dr. Seuss and Mr. Geisel*, 149.
32. Dr. Seuss, "Prayer for a Child," *Collier's*, December 1955, 86.
33. Morgan and Morgan, *Dr. Seuss and Mr. Geisel*, 182.
34. Ibid., 193.
35. Ibid., 202.
36. Ibid., 85.
37. Ibid., 195–96.

FIVE

1. Judith Morgan and Neil Morgan, *Dr. Seuss and Mr. Geisel: A Biography* (New York: Random House, 1995), 195.
2. Ibid., 198.
3. Ibid., 201.
4. Ibid., 263.
5. Dr. Seuss, *Did I Ever Tell You How Lucky You Are?* (New York: Random House, 1973).
6. Dr. Seuss, *Hunches in Bunches* (New York: Random House, 1982).
7. Dr. Seuss, *You're Only Old Once!* (New York: Random House, 1986).
8. Selma G. Lanes, "Seuss for the Goose Is Seuss for the Gander," in *Down the Rabbit Hole: Realism and Misadventures in the Realm of Children's Literature* (New York: Atheneum, 1971), 82.
9. Morgan and Morgan, *Dr. Seuss and Mr. Geisel*, 210.
10. Dr. Seuss, *The Lorax* (New York: Random House, 1971).
11. Morgan and Morgan, *Dr. Seuss and Mr. Geisel*, 211.
12. Ibid., 206.
13. Art Buchwald, syndicated column, July 30, 1974.
14. Morgan and Morgan, *Dr. Seuss and Mr. Geisel*, 221.
15. Ibid., 234–35.
16. Ibid., 276, 286.
17. Ibid., 249.
18. Dr. Seuss, *The Butter Battle Book* (New York: Random House, 1984).
19. Morgan and Morgan, *Dr. Seuss and Mr. Geisel*, 252–55.
20. Ibid., 276.
21. Jack Webb, "Dr. Seuss Also Has Worn Many Hats," *San Diego Tribune*, September 11, 1974, 21.

22. Karla Kuskin, "Seuss at 75," *New York Times Book Review*, April 29, 1979, cited in Morgan and Morgan, *Dr. Seuss and Mr. Geisel*, 245.

23. Michael Bandler, "Dr. Seuss Still a Drawing Card," *American Way*, December 1977.

24. Janet Shulman is quoted on http://www.seussville.com/.

25. Glenn Edward Sadler, "Maurice Sendak and Dr. Seuss: A Conversation," in *Of Sneetches and Whos and the Good Dr. Seuss: Essays on the Writing and Life of Theodor Geisel*, ed. Thomas Fensch (Jefferson, NC: McFarland, 1997), 139.

26. Michael Frith, "Dr. Seuss at Home," *Children's Book Cranny*, January–April 1973.

27. Morgan and Morgan, *Dr. Seuss and Mr. Geisel*, 286.

INDEX

Abel, Curtis, *33*
advertising
    for alcohol producers, 51
    post-war exploration of, 73
    requirements of, 74
    for Standard Oil, 48
    success in, 51
aging, 136
alcohol
    incident at Dartmouth, 35–38
    as topic of humor, 32, 44–45
    See also brewery business of Geisel
        family; Prohibition
ambivalence of Geisel, 18
American Can Company, 51
anapests, 110–11
And to Think That I Saw It on
    Mulberry Street
    on ability to make-believe, 19–20
    acquired by Random House, 143
    audience of, 18–20
    and childhood memories of Geisel,
        13
    depiction of hometown, 6–7
    and discontent of child protagonist,
        103
    and feminist critics, 143
    fiftieth anniversary of, 12
    in Japan and Korea, 93
    and memories of WWI, 51
    and *Oh, the Places You'll Go*, 151
    and parents of Geisel, 9–10, 19
    publication of, 24–25
    and racial stereotypes, 143
    reception of, 6–7, 23–24
    royalties from, 74

and Springfield cycle, 85
    story of, 7, 7–9, *8*
animal stories, 94. *See also specific*
    characters
animated cartoons, 69–70, 74, 90, 103
Anthony, Norman, 43
antiabortion activists, 141
anti-German sentiment
    and attitude toward minorities, 79
    development of, 14–15
    and humiliation felt by Geisel, 21,
        148
    and Marnie's agoraphobia, 14,
        71–72
    memories of, 14–15, 16, 61, 148
    and political cartoon career, 66
    reaction of Geisel to, 18, 21, 63, 66,
        75, 79
    and satire, 18
anti-Semitism, *65*, 65, 118, 119
anxiety, 13
arms race, 144–45
artwork
    bedroom-wall caricatures, 11
    colors of, 134, 137
    dissociation from war mentality, 80
    exaggeration in, *28*, 28–29, *31*, 149
    flying cow, 41, 61, 151
    Geisel's explanation of, 149
    and Helen, 41, 61
    for *Jack-O-Lantern*, 28
    recognition of, 50
    reevaluation of, 79
    and Theophrastus (stuffed dog),
        11, 152
    work process of, 150